Genocide

OTHER BOOKS OF RELATED INTEREST

OPPOSING VIEWPOINTS SERIES
Africa
Human Nature
Human Rights
War

CONTEMPORARY ISSUES COMPANION
Ethnic Violence
War Crimes

CURRENT CONTROVERSIES SERIES
Hate Crimes
Minorities
Nationalism and Ethnic Conflict
Violence Against Women

AT ISSUE SERIES
Anti-Semitism
Ethnic Conflict
The Militia Movement
The United Nations

Genocide

Bonnie Szumski, *Editorial Director*
Scott Barbour, *Managing Editor*
Brenda Stalcup, *Series Editor*
William Dudley, *Book Editor*

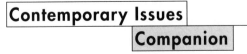

Contemporary Issues
Companion

Greenhaven Press, Inc., San Diego, CA

Library of Congress Cataloging-in-Publication Data

Genocide / William Dudley, book editor.
    p. cm. — (Contemporary issues companion)
    Includes bibliographical references and index.
    ISBN 0-7377-0680-5 (pbk. : alk. paper) —
ISBN 0-7377-0681-3 (lib. : alk. paper)
    1. Genocide. 2. Genocide—Case studies.
3. Genocide—Prevention. I. Dudley, William, 1964–
II. Series.

HV6322.7 .G48 2001
304.6'63—dc21   2001016143
                                                      CIP

©2001 by Greenhaven Press, Inc.
P.O. Box 289009, San Diego, CA 92198-9009

Printed in the U.S.A.

CONTENTS

FOREWORD

In the news, on the streets, and in neighborhoods, individuals are confronted with a variety of social problems. Such problems may affect people directly: A young woman may struggle with depression, suspect a friend of having bulimia, or watch a loved one battle cancer. And even the issues that do not directly affect her private life—such as religious cults, domestic violence, or legalized gambling—still impact the larger society in which she lives. Discovering and analyzing the complexities of issues that encompass communal and societal realms as well as the world of personal experience is a valuable educational goal in the modern world.

Effectively addressing social problems requires familiarity with a constantly changing stream of data. Becoming well informed about today's controversies is an intricate process that often involves reading myriad primary and secondary sources, analyzing political debates, weighing various experts' opinions—even listening to firsthand accounts of those directly affected by the issue. For students and general observers, this can be a daunting task because of the sheer volume of information available in books, periodicals, on the evening news, and on the Internet. Researching the consequences of legalized gambling, for example, might entail sifting through congressional testimony on gambling's societal effects, examining private studies on Indian gaming, perusing numerous websites devoted to Internet betting, and reading essays written by lottery winners as well as interviews with recovering compulsive gamblers. Obtaining valuable information can be time-consuming—since it often requires researchers to pore over numerous documents and commentaries before discovering a source relevant to their particular investigation.

Greenhaven's Contemporary Issues Companion series seeks to assist this process of research by providing readers with useful and pertinent information about today's complex issues. Each volume in this anthology series focuses on a topic of current interest, presenting informative and thought-provoking selections written from a wide variety of viewpoints. The readings selected by the editors include such diverse sources as personal accounts and case studies, pertinent factual and statistical articles, and relevant commentaries and overviews. This diversity of sources and views, found in every Contemporary Issues Companion, offers readers a broad perspective in one convenient volume.

In addition, each title in the Contemporary Issues Companion series is designed especially for young adults. The selections included in every volume are chosen for their accessibility and are expertly edited in consideration of both the reading and comprehension levels of the audience. The structure of the anthologies also enhances accessibility. An introductory essay places each issue in context and provides helpful facts such as historical background or current statistics and legislation that pertain to the topic. The chapters that follow organize the material and focus on specific aspects of the book's topic. Every essay is introduced by a brief summary of its main points and biographical information about the author. These summaries aid in comprehension and can also serve to direct readers to material of immediate interest and need. Finally, a comprehensive index allows readers to efficiently scan and locate content.

The Contemporary Issues Companion series is an ideal launching point for research on a particular topic. Each anthology in the series is composed of readings taken from an extensive gamut of resources, including periodicals, newspapers, books, government documents, the publications of private and public organizations, and Internet websites. In these volumes, readers will find factual support suitable for use in reports, debates, speeches, and research papers. The anthologies also facilitate further research, featuring a book and periodical bibliography and a list of organizations to contact for additional information.

A perfect resource for both students and the general reader, Greenhaven's Contemporary Issues Companion series is sure to be a valued source of current, readable information on social problems that interest young adults. It is the editors' hope that readers will find the Contemporary Issues Companion series useful as a starting point to formulate their own opinions about and answers to the complex issues of the present day.

INTRODUCTION

The word "genocide" first appeared in print in 1944 in the book *Axis Rule in Occupied Europe* by Raphael Lemkin, a Jewish lawyer and political refugee from Nazi-occupied Poland. Lemkin's goal was to alert America as to what was happening to the Jewish population in areas of Europe that were under the occupation of Nazi Germany. He wrote that the Nazis had instituted a systematic program designed to eliminate the Jews as a group. To fully describe this type of organized killing, Lemkin coined a new word, genocide, by combining the Greek word *genos* (race or tribe) with the Latin suffix *cide* (to kill). "Genocide," he wrote in a 1945 article,

> does not necessarily signify mass killings although it may mean that. More often it refers to a coordinated plan aimed at destruction of the essential foundations of the life of national groups. . . . Genocide is directed against a national group as an entity and the attack on individuals is only secondary to the annihilation of the national group to which they belong.

After the end of World War II and the full exposure of the horrors of Nazi death camps to the world, Lemkin helped spearhead a campaign calling for the international community to outlaw genocide and to take steps to prevent future Holocausts. In 1946 the fledgling United Nations (U.N.) declared genocide—both in times of war and of peace—to be a crime against humanity. In 1948 the United Nations passed the Convention on the Prevention and Punishment of the Crime of Genocide, which defined genocide as "acts committed with intent to destroy, in whole or in part, a national, ethnical, racial or religious group." These acts could encompass not only killing members of a targeted group, but also creating living conditions designed to bring about the destruction of a group, preventing births within a group, or forcibly removing children of the targeted group to be brought up by another ethnic or national group. Nations who signed the convention committed themselves under international law to prevent genocide from occurring and to punish perpetrators of genocide.

The convention went into effect in 1951, when it was ratified by sixty nations. However, for the first forty years of its existence, the convention was generally ignored by the world community. Scholar Claude W. Welch asserts that between 1945 and 1980 alone, more individuals were killed in forty-three separate genocides than by outright warfare. Nevertheless, during this period no nation cited the 1948 U.N. convention as a reason for intervening in another country, no individuals were captured or indicted for committing genocide, and no official international tribunals were created to investigate or punish genocidal acts. According to Samantha Power, director of the Human Rights Initiative at the Kennedy School of Government in Harvard University, while "the Genocide Convention initially succeeded in articulating a postwar international consensus that genocide was a monstrous evil, neither it nor the rhetorical commitments of the American leaders . . . translated into a willingness to halt the masterminds of genocide."

One possible explanation for the failure of the United Nations to prevent further Holocausts during this time was the Cold War between the United States and the Soviet Union. These two nations with ideologically opposed systems of government emerged from World War II as the world's most powerful countries. They were soon locked in an intense global competition for influence—one that divided the world into Soviet and American blocs. Enforcement of the U.N. convention against genocide took a back seat in American foreign policy to such concerns as cultivating alliances, halting the spread of communism, decreasing the influence of the Soviet Union, and preventing nuclear war. In addition, as members of the U.N. Security Council, both nations held the right to veto U.N. actions, and they often used this prerogative to veto policies favored by the other superpower. The two Cold War adversaries thus effectively precluded any prospect of united and effective U.N. military intervention in situations of genocide.

The collapse of the Soviet Union in 1991 and the end of the Cold War changed the international landscape and helped to revive the viability of U.N. action against genocide. It is in all likelihood no coincidence that the 1990s—the first decade after the Cold War—was when the United States and United Nations began to take some steps to enforce the convention against genocide, primarily in the former Yugoslavia and Rwanda. Following its breakup in the early 1990s, the former Yugoslavia became engulfed in war for several years, during which ethnic Serbs were accused of forcibly removing and massacring members of other ethnic and religious groups, including Croats and Bosnian Muslims. In the small African nation of Rwanda, ethnic hostilities culminated in genocidal actions in 1994, when the Rwandan government and military targeted ethnic Tutsi for elimination. The world community's response to these events helped place genocide closer to the forefront of international affairs. However, the problems that arose demonstrated that despite the end of the Cold War, impediments remain that prevent the full implementation of the 1948 Genocide Convention.

One obstacle to effective U.N. action stems from difficulties in determining whether genocide is taking place, and especially in distinguishing genocide from the violence endemic in warfare and civil conflict. Warfare within states that does not involve the targeted elimination of a specific ethnic group triggers no obligation under the

1948 Genocide Convention for foreign intervention. In both the former Yugoslavia and in Rwanda, genocidal acts took place within the context of civil war, making it difficult for outside observers to discern when the violence was genocidal in nature. Genocide scholars such as Helen Fein have noted that looking at a possible genocide through the lens of civil war can change how it is perceived in the rest of the world. As Fein explains, such framing "mitigates against viewing and labeling these acts as international crimes . . . and forestalls drawing on moral or legal obligations to stop them." Those accused of genocide in both Yugoslavia and in Rwanda have attempted to use this perception to their advantage. "It is no coincidence that [former Yugoslav president] Slobodan Milosevic consistently referred to the war he unleashed against the newly independent states of the former Yugoslavia as a 'civil war'," writes *Human Rights Review* editor Thomas Cushman. "To the extent that this definition of the situation became dominant, it became harder for those who had experienced the crime of genocide (in this case, the Bosnian Muslims) to press their case and seek justice."

Another, perhaps more important, impediment against effective international action against genocide is the reluctance of the United States and other countries to place their own soldiers at risk in a military intervention. Power states, "The most common justification for non-intervention is that, while leaving genocide alone threatens no vital American interests, suppressing it can threaten the lives of American soldiers." This hesitation was evident in the cases of both Yugoslavia and Rwanda. In Yugoslavia, U.S. officials limited direct intervention to air strikes as a way of minimizing American casualties. In Rwanda, a U.N. peacekeeping force stationed there was quickly withdrawn after some of its soldiers were killed by the Rwandan military; the United Nations and the United States subsequently did little to intervene in the genocide that followed. Both the United States and the United Nations have been criticized for not taking stronger measures to stop genocides in progress. "Robust suppression via substantial and decisive military force is the *key* to stopping genocide," insists scholar Kenneth J. Campbell. But such force is rarely implemented, he maintains: "Political leaders, designated the stopping of genocide as a less-than-vital national interest, and assuming their domestic policies would not tolerate military casualties among their own troops to stop genocide, opted for far less effective methods." While the world community may have responded to the genocidal acts in Yugoslavia and Rwanda to a greater extent than in similar crises in prior decades, Campbell and other critics argue that far greater intervention is necessary.

Nations' obligations under the 1948 Genocide Convention encompass not only suppressing genocides when they occur, but also punishing those individuals responsible for the perpetration of genocides.

Progress has been made in carrying out this goal since the end of the Cold War, but whether enough has been done is a matter of debate. An international criminal tribunal was envisaged, but not mandated, by the writers of the convention. However, the United Nations did not create the first tribunal to implement the convention until 1993, when the International Criminal Tribunal for the former Yugoslavia (ICTY) was formed to deal with genocide and other crimes against humanity committed there since 1991. Another ad hoc tribunal—the International Criminal Tribunal for Rwanda (ICTR)—was created in the following year. Both tribunals incorporated the definition of genocide set forth in the 1948 convention in their statutes.

On September 2, 1998, Jean-Paul Akayesu, a former mayor in Rwanda, became the first individual to be convicted of genocide under the 1948 convention. In 1999, the Yugoslav tribunal indicted Milosevic and several other Yugoslav leaders. Some commentators have praised these tribunals, citing their actions as evidence that the international community is living up to its obligation to punish genocide. However, as of the end of 2000, Milsosevic and others indicted by the ICTY had yet to even be arrested. The tribunal in Rwanda has also been criticized for its slow pace and lack of resources. International criminal justice scholar George S. Yacoubian Jr. concluded in 1999 that "if successful international criminal justice is measured in terms of concrete results, the ICTR has clearly failed." Whether the performance of these tribunals will improve with experience over time remains to be seen.

The selections in *Genocide: Contemporary Issues Companion* examine the issues concerning what the United States and other nations should do to prevent and punish genocide. Other chapters cover past genocides of the twentieth century, including the Holocaust, and investigate the social and psychological reasons why genocides occur. A final chapter discusses the concept of "cultural genocide" and the contemporary plight of many ethnic groups whose physical and/or cultural survival is threatened by war, government policies, and economic modernization. The articles in this volume both look back to the twentieth century, a time when millions of people perished in genocides, and look forward to the twenty-first in the hopes that such atrocities will never occur again.

CHAPTER 1

GENOCIDE IN THE TWENTIETH CENTURY

THE ARMENIAN GENOCIDE

The California State Department of Education

For five centuries, the Armenians, a predominately Christian ethnic group, lived within the Ottoman Empire, a multiethnic domain ruled by Muslim Turks. Then, beginning in 1915, Turkish reformers within the Ottoman Empire embarked on a crusade to eliminate its Armenian minority. Over the next several years between a half million and two million Armenians were killed; the rest were forcibly removed from their traditional homeland. The following essay, which was produced by the California State Department of Education, provides a brief history of the Armenian genocide and draws comparisons between it and the genocidal campaigns of Nazi Germany during World War II.

The general public and even many historians know very little about the genocide of Armenians by the government of the Ottoman Empire. Civilian populations have often fallen victim to the brutality of invading armies, bombing raids, lethal substances, and other forms of indiscriminate killings. In the Armenian case, however, the government of the Ottoman Empire, dominated by the so-called Committee of Union and Progress or Young Turk Party, turned against a segment of its own population. In international law there were certain accepted laws and customs of war that were aimed in some measure at protecting civilian populations, but these did not cover domestic situations or a government's treatment of its own people. Only after World War II and the Holocaust was that aspect included in the United Nations' Genocide Convention. Nonetheless, at the time of the Armenian deportations and massacres beginning in 1915, many governments and statespersons termed the atrocities as crimes against humanity.

Except for the Young Turk leaders, no government denied or doubted what was occurring. The governments of Germany and Austro-Hungary, while allied with the Ottoman Empire, received hundreds of detailed eyewitness accounts from their officials on the spot and privately admitted that the Armenians were being subjected to a policy of annihilation. In the United States charity drives began for the remnants of the "starving Armenians." Examples of

Excerpted from the California State Department of Education, "Appendix B," in *Model Curriculum for Human Rights and Genocide.* Copyright © 1987 the California State Department of Education.

headlines from the *New York Times* in 1915 read: "[Ambassador Morgenthau] Protests Against the War of Extermination in Progress" (September 16); "Only 200,000 Armenians Now Left in Turkey: More than 1,000,000 Killed, Enslaved, or Exiled" (October 22); "Five Missionaries Succumb to Shock of Armenian Horrors" (November 3); "Million Armenians Killed or in Exile: American Committee on Relief Says. Victims . . . Steadily Increasing" (December 15). Between 1915 and 1918, hundreds of declarations, promises, and pledges were made by world leaders regarding the emancipation, restitution, and rehabilitation of the Armenian survivors. Yet, within a few years those same governments and statespersons turned away from the Armenian question without having fulfilled any of those pledges. And, after a few more years, the Armenian calamity had virtually become "the forgotten genocide."

The History of the Armenians

The Armenians are an ancient people. They inhabited the highland region between the Black, Caspian, and Mediterranean Seas for nearly 3,000 years. They are noted in Greek and Persian sources as early as the sixth century B.C. On a strategic crossroad between East and West, Armenia was sometimes independent under its national dynasties, sometimes autonomous under native princes who paid tribute to foreign powers, and sometimes subjected to direct foreign rule. The Armenians were among the first people to adopt Christianity and to develop a distinct national-religious culture.

The Turkish invasions of Armenia began in the eleventh century A.D., and the last Armenian kingdom fell three centuries later. Most of the territories that had once formed the ancient and medieval Armenian kingdoms were incorporated into the Ottoman Empire in the sixteenth century. The Armenians were included in a multinational and multireligious realm, but as a Christian minority they had to endure official discrimination and second-class citizenship, including special taxes, inadmissibility of legal testimony, and the prohibition on bearing arms.

Despite these disabilities, most Armenians lived in relative peace so long as the Ottoman Empire was strong and expanding. But as the empire's administrative, fiscal, and military structure crumbled under the weight of internal corruption and external challenges in the eighteenth and nineteenth centuries, oppression and intolerance increased. The breakdown of order was accelerated by Ottoman inability to modernize and compete with the West.

The decay of the Ottoman Empire was paralleled by cultural and political revival among many of the subject peoples. The national liberation struggles, supported at times by one or another European power, resulted in Turkish loss of Greece and most of the Balkan provinces in the nineteenth century and aggravated the Eastern Question; that is, what was to happen to the enervated empire and its constituent peoples. A growing number of Ottoman liberals came to believe that the empire's survival depended on effective administration reforms. These men were movers behind several significant reform measures promulgated between 1839 and 1876. Yet time and again the advocates of reform became disillusioned in the face of the entrenched, vested interests that stubbornly resisted change.

Of the various subject peoples, the Armenians perhaps sought the least. Unlike the Balkan Christians or the Arabs, they were dispersed throughout the empire and no longer constituted an absolute majority in much of their historic homelands. Hence, most Armenian leaders did not think in terms of independence. Expressing loyalty to the sultan and disavowing any separatist aspirations, they petitioned for the protection of their people and property from corrupt officials and marauding bands. The Armenians had passed through a long period of cultural revival. Thousands of youngsters enrolled in elementary and secondary schools, and hundreds of students traveled to Europe for higher education. Many returned home imbued with ideas of the Enlightenment and the French Revolution to engage in teaching, journalism, and literary criticism. As it happened, however, this Armenian self-discovery was paralleled by heightened administrative corruption and exploitation. It was this dual development, the conscious demand for enlightened government and security of life on the one hand and the growing repression and insecurity on the other, that gave rise to the Armenian Question as a part of the larger Eastern Question. Some Armenians gave up hope that reforms could be achieved peaceably. They organized underground political parties and encouraged the population to learn to defend itself.

Massacres: Preface to Genocide

During the reign of Sultan Abdul-Hamid II (1876–1909), a new reform measure relating specifically to the Armenians was promulgated under pressure from the European powers. However, European interest was inconsistent, and foreign intervention unsustained by effective measures to oversee the implementation of the reforms only compounded Armenian troubles. Beginning in the mountainous district of Sassun in 1894 and then spreading to every province inhabited by Armenians in 1895 and 1896, pogroms organized by the sultan's agents resulted in the deaths of up to 200,000 Armenians, the flight into exile of thousands more, and the looting and burning or forced conversion of hundreds of towns and villages. . . .

The sultan's use of violent methods was a desperate attempt to maintain the status quo in the face of severe external and internal challenges. In this regard, a major difference between Abdul-Hamid and his Young Turk successors was that he unleashed massacres in an effort to preserve a state structure in which the Armenians would be kept submissive and unable to resist tyrannical rule, whereas the Young Turks were to employ the same tactics on a much grander scale to bring about fundamental and far-reaching changes in the status quo and create an entirely new frame of reference that did not include the Armenians at all.

The Young Turk Dictatorship

Disillusion weighed heavily on the Armenians after the calamities of 1894–1896, yet some comfort was found in the fact that various non-Armenian elements were also trying to organize against the sultan's tyranny. Several of those opposition groups merged into the Committee of Union and Progress, popularly referred to as the Young Turks. In 1908 a military coup led by the Young Turks forced Abdul-Hamid to become a constitutional monarch. The Armenians hailed the victory of Young Turks amid manifestations of Christian and Muslim Ottoman brotherhood.

From 1908–1914 the seemingly egalitarian Young Turks became xenophobic nationalists bent on creating a new order and eliminating the Armenian Question by eliminating the Armenian people. European exploitation of Turkish weaknesses after the 1908 revolution and the Turkish loss of more territory in the Balkans contributed to this process. In 1909 more than 20,000 Armenians were massacred in the region of Cilicia. The Young Turks blamed Abdul-Hamid and deposed him, but there were strong indications that adherents of the Young Turks had themselves participated in the carnage. The crisis prompted the Young Turks to declare a state of siege and suspend constitutional rights for several years.

It was during this period that the concept of "Turkism" and exclusive nationalism attracted several prominent Young Turks, who began to envisage a new, homogeneous Turkish state in place of the enervated and exploited multinational Ottoman Empire. With the ideology of Turkism expounded by writers such as Zia Gokalp, the Young Turk extremists began to contemplate ways to abandon multinational "Ottomanism" for exclusivist "Turkism" and so transform the Ottoman Empire into a homogeneous Turkish domain. . . .

The outbreak of World War I in the summer of 1914 deeply alarmed the Armenians. If the Ottoman Empire entered the conflict on the side of Germany, the Armenian plateau would become the inevitable theater of another Russo-Turkish war. In view of the fact that the Armenian homelands lay on both sides of the frontier, the Armenians would suffer severely no matter who might eventually win the war. For these reasons, Armenian spokespersons implored the Young Turk leaders to maintain neutrality and spare the empire from disaster. Despite these appeals, the Germanophile Young Turk faction, led by Minister of War Enver Pasha and Minister of Internal Affairs Talaat Pasha, sealed a secret alliance with Berlin and in return for joining the war against Great Britain, France, and Russia, looked to the creation of a new Turkish realm extending into Central Asia. The Armenians were now seen as an obstacle to the realization of that goal. Turkism was to supplant Ottomanism and give purpose and justification to unlimited violence for the greater good of producing a homogeneous state and society. In *Accounting for Genocide,* Helen Fein concluded:

> The victims of twentieth century premeditated genocide—the Jew, the Gypsies, the Armenians—were murdered in order to fulfill the state's design for a new order. . . . War was used in both cases . . . to transform the nation to correspond to the ruling elite's formula by eliminating the groups conceived as alien, enemies by definition.

The Genocidal Process

On the night of April 23–24, 1915, Armenian political, religious, educational, and intellectual leaders in Constantinople (Istanbul) were arrested, deported into Anatolia, and put to death. In May, after mass deportations had already begun, Minister of Internal Affairs Talaat Pasha, claiming that the Armenians were untrustworthy, could offer aid and comfort to the enemy, and were in a state of imminent rebellion, ordered *ex post facto* their deportation from the war zones to relocation centers—actually the barren deserts of Syria and Mesopotamia. The Armenians were driven out, not only from areas near war zones but from the length and breadth of the empire, except in Constantinople and Smyrna, where numerous foreign diplomats and merchants were located. Sometimes Armenian Catholics and Protestants were exempted from the deportation decrees, only to follow once the majority belonging to the Armenian Apostolic Church had been dispatched. Secrecy, surprise, and deception were all part of the process.

The whole of Asia Minor was put in motion. Armenians serving in the Ottoman armies had already been segregated into unarmed labor battalions and were now taken out in batches and murdered. Of the remaining population, the adult and teenage males were, as a pattern, swiftly separated from the deportation caravans and killed outright under the direction of Young Turk agents, the gendarmerie, and bandit and nomadic groups prepared for the operation. Women and children were driven for months over mountains and deserts. Intentionally deprived of food and water, they fell by the thousands and the hundreds of thousands along the routes to the desert. In this manner the Armenian people were effectively eliminated from their homeland of several millennia. Of the refugee survivors scattered throughout the Arab provinces and the Caucasus, thousands more were to die of starvation, epidemic, and exposure. Even the memory of the nation was intended for obliteration, as churches and cultural monuments were desecrated and small children, snatched from their parents, were renamed and given out to be raised as non-Armenians and non-Christians. . . .

Henry Morgenthau Sr., the American Ambassador to Turkey at the time, tried to reason with the Young Turk leaders and to alert the United States and the world to the tragic events, but, except for some donations for relief efforts, his actions were in vain. His description of the genocide begins:

> The Central Government now announced its intention of gathering the two million or more Armenians living in the several sections of the empire and transporting them to this desolate and inhospitable region. Had they undertaken such a deportation in good faith, it would have represented the height of cruelty and injustice. As a matter of fact, the Turks never had the slightest idea of reestablishing the Armenians in this new country. . . . The real purpose of the deportation was robbery and destruction; it really represented a new method of massacre. When the Turkish authorities gave the orders for these deportations, they were merely giving the death warrant to the whole race; they understood this well, and, in their conversations with me, they made no particular attempt to conceal the fact.

Ambassador Morgenthau concluded:

> I am confident that the whole history of the human race contains no terrible episode as this.

Estimates of the Armenian dead vary from 600,000 to two million. A United Nations Human Rights Subcommission report in 1985 gives the figure of "at least one million," but the important point in understanding a tragedy such as this is not the exact and precise count of the number who died—that will never be known—but the fact that more than half the Armenian population perished and the rest were forcibly driven from their ancestral homeland. Another important point is that what befell the Armenians was by the will of the government. While a large segment of the general population participated in the looting and massacres, many Muslim leaders were shocked by what was happening, and thousands of Armenian women and children were rescued and sheltered by compassionate individual Turks, Kurds, and Arabs.

Although the decimation of the Armenian people and the destruction of millions of persons in Central and Eastern Europe during the Nazi regime a quarter of a century later each had particular and unique features, there were some striking parallels. The similarities include the perpetration of genocide under the cover of a major international conflict, thus minimizing the possibility of external

intervention; conception of the plan by a monolithic and xenophobic clique; espousal of an ideology giving purpose and justification to
racism, exclusivism, and intolerance toward elements resisting or
deemed unworthy of assimilation; imposition of strict party discipline and secrecy during the period of preparation; formation of
extralegal special armed forces to ensure the rigorous execution of
the operation; provocation of public hostility toward the victim
group and ascribing to it the very excesses to which it would be subjected; certainty of the vulnerability of the targeted groups (demonstrated in the Armenian case by the previous massacres of 1894–1896
and 1909); exploitation of advances in mechanization and commu-
nication to achieve uprecedented means for control, coordination,
and thoroughness; and the use of sanctions such as promotions and
incentive to loot or, conversely, the dismissal and punishment of
reluctant officials and the intimidation of persons who might consider harboring members of the victim group.

The Aftermath

The defeat of the Ottoman Empire and its allies at the end of 1918
raised the possibility of enacting the numerous pledges concerning
the punishment of the perpetrators and the rehabilitation of the
Armenian survivors. After the Young Turk leaders had fled the country, the new Turkish prime minister admitted that the Turks had committed such misdeeds "as to make the conscience of mankind shud-
der forever." United States General James G. Harbord, after an
inspection tour of the former Armenian population centers in 1919,
reported on the organized nature of the massacres and concluded:
"Mutilation, violation, torture, and death have left their haunting
memories in a hundred beautiful Armenian valleys, and the traveler
in that region is seldom free from the evidence of this most colossal
crime of all the ages." The Paris Peace Conference declared that the
lands of Armenia would never be returned to Turkish rule, and a Turkish military court-martial tried and sentenced to death in absentia
Enver, Talaat, [Navy Minister Jemal] Pasha, and [Education Minister
Nazim] Bey, notorious organizers of the genocide. No attempt was
made to carry out the sentence, however, and thousands of other culprits were neither tried nor even removed from office. Within a few
months the judicial proceedings were suspended, and even accused
and imprisoned war criminals were freed and sent home.

The release of the perpetrators of genocide signaled a major shift in
the political winds. The former Allied Powers, having become bitter
rivals over the spoils of war, failed to act in unison in imposing peace
or in dealing with the stiff resistance of a Turkish nationalist movement. They concurred that the Armenians should be freed and reha-
bilitated but took no effective measure to achieve that objective. They
hoped that the United States would extend a protectorate over the

devastated Armenian regions, but the United States was recoiling from its involvement in the world war and turning its back on the League of Nations. Unable to quell the Turkish nationalist movement, which rejected the award of any territory for an Armenian state or even unrestricted return of the Armenian refugees, the Allied Powers in 1923 made their peace with the new Turkey. No provision was made for the rehabilitation, restitution, or compensation of the Armenian survivors. Western abandonment of the Armenians was so complete that the revised peace treaties included no mention whatsoever of "Armenians" or "Armenia." It was as if the Armenians had never existed in the Ottoman Empire. All Armenians who had returned to their homes after the war were again uprooted and driven into exile. The 3,000-year presence of the Armenians in Asia Minor came to a violent end. Armenian place-names were changed, and Armenian cultural monuments were obliterated or allowed to fall into disrepair. Attempts to eliminate the memory of Armenia included change of the geographical expression "Armenian plateau" to "Eastern Anatolia." The Armenian survivors were condemned to a life of exile and dispersion, being subjected to inevitable acculturation and assimilation on five continents and facing an increasingly indifferent world. With the consolidation of totalitarian regimes in Europe during the 1920s and 1930s, memory of the Armenian cataclysm gradually faded, and in the aftermath of the horrors and havoc of World War II, it virtually became the "forgotten genocide."

In recent years, growing awareness of the Holocaust and commitment to the prevention and punishment of the crime of genocide has again raised the Armenian Genocide to the level of consciousness among educators, scholars, and defenders of human rights. The transgenerational trauma of the Armenian people is beginning to be understood, and various official and unofficial bodies have called on the present government of the Republic of Turkey to recognize the injustice perpetrated against the Armenians by previous Turkish governments.

Why Remember?

Students must learn the importance of and reasons for remembering the genocide of the Armenians by the government of the Ottoman Empire. They should consider whether it is possible for dispossessed peoples who have no sovereign state or government of their own to place their case before national and international bodies that operate within the framework of nation-states. How is it possible to seek legal recourse, to have truth prevail over perceived national interests, and to liberate history from politics?

In a thoughtful essay, Terrence Des Pres, author of *The Survivor: An Anatomy of Life in the Death Camps* and member of the United States Holocaust Council, has captured the importance of remembering:

Milan Kundera, the exiled Czech novelist, has written that "the struggle of man against power is the struggle of memory against forgetting." This single remark, in my view, sums up the human predicament today and puts the burden of responsibility exactly where it falls—on writers, and now more than ever, on scholars. . . . National catastrophes can be survived if (and perhaps only if) those to whom disaster happens can recover themselves through knowing the truth of their suffering. Great powers, on the other hand, would vanquish not only the peoples they subjugate but also the cultural mechanism that would sustain vital memory of historical crimes.

When modern states make way for geopolitical power plays, they are not above removing everything—nations, cultures, homelands—in their paths. Great powers regularly demolish other peoples' claims to dignity and place, and sometimes, as we know, the outcome is genocide. In a very real sense, therefore, Kundera is right: Against historical crimes we fight as best we can, and a cardinal part of this engagement is "the struggle of memory against forgetting."

HITLER'S FINAL SOLUTION

Doris L. Bergen

The most infamous genocide of the twentieth century was the mass extermination of Jews and Gypsies by Nazi Germany under Adolf Hitler. Hitler espoused the belief that "Aryan" Germans were a superior race whose nation had been weakened by "racially undesirable" groups such as the Jews. Following Hitler's accession to power in 1933, German Jews were subjected to increasingly harsh policies, including deprivation of political and civil rights, segregation into ghettos, and forced emigration. Germany's early successes in World War II brought millions of European Jews from various countries under Nazi control. As historian Doris L. Bergen explains in the following selection, in 1941 Hitler decided to implement a "final solution" to the "Jewish problem"—the Holocaust—that resulted in the death of six million Jews.

The "Final Solution" is a Nazi term. It refers to the program, implemented during World War II, to solve what the Nazis called the "Jewish Problem." There was of course no problem, other than the fact that Nazi ideology denied Jews the right to exist. The Nazi "solution" was mass murder, an attempt to kill all the Jews of Europe, and eventually of the entire world. It was not just Hitler and his elite troops, the SS, who committed genocide. The German government bureaucracy, the military, the educational system, doctors, scientists, parents, pastors, judges, camp guards, women and men of all ages were needed to make the Holocaust a reality. Between 1939 and 1945, they killed about six million Jews from all over Europe: Germany, Poland, the Netherlands, Hungary, Rumania, Greece, the Soviet Union, and anywhere else the Nazis gained control.

Efforts at supposed racial purification targeted other people as well as Jews. In processes closely related to the Final Solution, Nazis and their accomplices murdered over 70,000 Germans deemed handicapped and nearly half a million European Gypsies. They persecuted, tortured, and killed Soviet prisoners of war, Polish intellectuals, homosexual men, Jehovah's Witnesses, and Germans of African heritage. This essay examines the mechanisms of this program of destruction, with a focus on the largest and most systematically pursued group of victims: the Jews.

Case Study—Thaddeus Stabholz

In some ways, Thaddeus Stabholz typifies the experience of European Jews in the Holocaust. "Teddy" Stabholz grew up in a middle-class, assimilated Jewish family in Poland. In September 1939, when the Germans invaded Poland and World War II began in Europe, he was a young medical student in Warsaw. Months after the Germans defeated Poland, they forced Teddy, his father, his grandmother, and the rest of his relatives, like Jews all over the country, to move into a ghetto. Ghettos were designated parts of cities where Jews lived in cramped quarters, cut off from the outside world. The Stabholzes moved into the Warsaw ghetto. Teddy's mother had died in 1938 of cancer; in 1941, his father was killed by Germans.

Teddy was left alone "like a homeless dog," he wrote later. With his fiancée Fredzia he survived as best he could on the food they could scrounge. Teddy cared for his grandmother, too, until January 1943 when Nazis beat her to death on the street. By that time, many of the Jews—especially the old, very young, and sick—had already been taken out of the ghetto and killed in the gas chambers at the death camp Treblinka.

In early 1943, some of the young Jews left in the Warsaw ghetto organized an uprising against the Germans. Teddy and Fredzia were among them. They fought desperately with whatever weapons they had, but they were no match for the SS firepower. The Germans burned the ghetto, killed most of the people still in it, and sent the remaining few to Treblinka. There Fredzia was murdered, as were about one million other Jews, many of them from Warsaw. For some unknown reason, Teddy was sent on to Majdanek, a labor camp as well as a killing center. He remained a prisoner of the Nazis for the next two years, until the Allies defeated Germany in the spring of 1945.

Through extraordinary luck, Teddy Stabholz survived. Guards selected him to be killed at Majdanek but at the last minute pulled him out of the group and made him a medic. At Auschwitz-Birkenau he was starved, beaten, and forced to carry enormous loads of water and cement at the double for miles. He almost died of pneumonia. For a time he even had a "job" delousing the body hair of fellow prisoners with Zyklon B (hydrogen cyanide)—the same insecticide used in the gas chambers to murder millions of people. Stabholz managed to win the favor of some senior prisoners and guards by "operating" on the corns and callouses on their feet. In the summer of 1944, he witnessed the murder of all the Gypsies in Auschwitz as the Germans prepared the camp to receive Jews from Hungary.

Late in 1944, as the Soviet Army approached Auschwitz, the Germans began to evacuate the camp. Stabholz was sent to a concentration camp called Sachsenhausen, not far from Berlin. As he heard the roar of Allied bombers overhead, Teddy began to hope for the first time that he might live to see the Nazi collapse. But he still faced months of excruciating work, plagues of typhus and lice, and transfers to camps further from the front lines. At one point, Teddy resigned himself to die. But a vision of his father and mother revived his will to live and encouraged him to fight on.

In April 1945, American troops fighting their way through southern Germany found Stabholz and some fellow prisoners who had escaped from the SS and hidden in the woods. After spending time in a displaced person's camp in Germany, Teddy came to the United States. He graduated from the University of Vermont's medical school and started a practice in Canton, Ohio, where he still lives today. Dr. Stabholz has two daughters (Stabholz, passim).

Murder of People Deemed Handicapped

One component of the Nazi program of mass murder began even before war broke out in September 1939: the murder of the handicapped. In 1938, a German woman named Knauer gave birth to a baby. Apparently it had severe handicaps, and the parents wrote to Hitler asking for permission to have doctors kill the child. Hitler used the case to move toward a goal he had long espoused: ridding Germany of what he and others called "lives unworthy of living"—the mentally and physically handicapped.

Hitler authorized his personal physician, Dr. Karl Brandt, and Philipp Bouhler, a high-ranking functionary in the Nazi Party, to organize the Children's "Euthanasia" Program. By the time the war started, the killing machinery was in place, and the program expanded to include adults as well. Its code name was "T-4." In the T-4 program the Nazis pioneered methods of mass killing, such as the use of poison gas in mobile units and gas chambers. They also trained personnel who would later be active in the genocide of the Jews. Most importantly, Hitler and his henchmen tested the reactions of the German public.

"Euthanasia" means mercy killing, but the T-4 program had nothing to do with mercy. Those selected for murder were not terminally ill nor did they or their families have any say in the decision. Social workers, doctors, and nurses provided information on people who had been institutionalized in hospitals and asylums, and teams of assessors decided who was to live and who to die. The assessors did not examine or usually even see the people whose fates they determined. Some health professionals refused to participate in the program, but Nazi authorities had no trouble finding enough ambitious doctors, nurses, administrators, and judges to cooperate. Patients selected for death were removed from their institutions and sent to specially designated "hospitals" for killing. The perpetrators used various methods. Sometimes the transport vehicles themselves were mobile gas chambers. In other cases, people were taken to killing centers and gassed, given lethal injections, or used in deadly "experiments."

It was impossible to keep the "euthanasia" program a secret. Workers in hospitals and mental institutions witnessed the "transfer" of patients who never returned. Even those people marked for death often learned in advance of their fate. One nurse told of a hospitalized woman who cried piteously while being led to the bus. "How can I help being as I am and that people are doing this to me?" she wanted to know (Noakes and Pridham, II: p. 1030). Children in the towns near the killing centers learned to recognize the distinctive buses with their blacked-out windows. Stop acting retarded, they taunted each other, or those vans will take you away.

The German public did not remain indifferent. Protests from bereaved families and friends reached Hitler's desk. Some Catholic and Protestant churchmen denounced the killings. The pope insisted that "the direct killing of an innocent person because of mental or physical defects is not allowed" (Noakes and Pridham, II: p. 1035). But the most powerful response came from the Catholic bishop of Münster, Cardinal August Count von Galen. In August 1941, von Galen preached a sermon that described the killing program in detail. "Woe to mankind," he concluded, "woe to our German nation if God's holy commandment 'Thou shalt not kill' . . . is not only broken, but if this transgression is actually tolerated and permitted to go unpunished" (Noakes and Pridham, II: p. 1038).

Thousands of copies of von Galen's sermon were distributed in Germany and abroad. Nazi authorities were furious but did not dare to arrest the popular bishop. Hitler called a halt to the T-4 program. Killings of the handicapped did not stop completely, but they continued on a smaller scale, further from the centers of German population. Von Galen's protest proved that popular opposition from Germans could make a difference. But no outcry from German citizens on a comparable scale occurred in the case of the murder of either the Gypsies or the Jews.

The Occupation of Poland

Hitler considered war a necessary step toward achieving his goals of "racial purity" and expansion of German "living space." In January 1939, in a speech to the German parliament, he even predicted that the next world war would mean "the annihilation of the Jewish race in Europe" (Jäckel, p. 61). And indeed, the outbreak of war in September 1939 and the subsequent defeat of Poland gave the Nazis new opportunities and new territory in which to implement their quest for a master race.

Germany's Jewish population was small, but about three million Jews lived in Poland. When German tanks and troops overran Poland in the fall of 1939, those Jews became the prime targets of Nazi brutality. Between 1939 and 1941, Germans stole the Polish Jews' property, confined them to ghettos, forced many into hard labor, starved, beat, and humiliated them. By 1941, when Hitler fixed on total extermination as the Final Solution to the "Jewish Problem," hundreds of thousands of Polish Jews had already been killed. The major death camps constructed in late 1941 and 1942 eradicated all but a few of the rest.

Before attacking Poland in 1939, Hitler and his foreign minister had taken the precaution of signing a nonaggression pact with the Soviet Union. When the Nazis marched in from the west, Soviet troops moved in from the other side to take over eastern Poland. Many Jews fled from the Germans to the Soviet-held territory. Two years later, when Germany invaded the Soviet Union, they fell into Nazi hands again. In the meantime, the Germans incorporated part of their half of Poland into the "German Reich" and ruled the remainder as a sort of colony called the *Generalgouvernement*. They planned massive transfers of people in the area in order to create "purely Aryan" German settlements. Polish gentiles were to be pushed to the east, and Polish Jews confined to a kind of reservation near Lublin.

Many Nazi authorities wanted a piece of the action in Poland. The German military believed that its victories earned it the say in the region. But Heinrich Himmler, Hitler's righthand man and head of the SS, insisted that his organization should reign supreme. Others vying for power included the governor Hans Frank, local Nazis, the German Interior Ministry, and Hermann Göring, Hitler's deputy and head of the four-year plan for the economy. All of them soon discovered that the way to distinguish themselves, expand their sphere of control, and win Hitler's approval was to be even harsher, more efficient, and more extreme than their competitors in persecuting the Polish population, especially the Jews.

Organizers from Germany urged local ethnic Germans to attack their Polish gentile and Jewish neighbors and steal their property. In late 1939, an ambitious bureaucrat named Adolf Eichmann in the Reich Security Main Office in Berlin organized transports of Jews from the German Reich to the *Generalgouvernement*. The Jews, rounded up from cities such as Vienna, were dumped in the Polish woods and told to disappear or they would be shot. German soldiers and especially the SS and German police in Poland declared open season on Jews. They raped women, singled out Orthodox men for special torments, and killed Jews of all ages for sport. Germans locked Jews in synagogues and cafés, forced their families and friends to pay ransoms, and often burned the buildings with the people inside anyway. They stirred up hatred between members of Poland's ethnic groups, paying Polish gentiles to identify their Jewish neighbors, and recruiting Ukrainians and White Russians as auxiliary police and accomplices in assaults on Polish gentiles and Jews.

Abuses reached the point where even some German military leaders complained to Hitler. Such undisciplined violence would damage

Germany's reputation abroad, they worried, and destroy their troops' morale. Hitler's response was typical. We won't win a war with Salvation Army tactics, he retorted. And in fact, protest fizzled in the spring of 1940, as German forces achieved one victory after another on the western front, conquering Denmark, Norway, the Netherlands, Belgium, and France. Now the Jews in those countries found themselves in German hands as well.

Ghettoization

In the Nazi mind, the "Jewish Problem" continued to expand as Germans occupied more and more of Europe. Some officials favored the so-called Madagascar Plan—deportation of all Jews to the island of Madagascar off the east coast of Africa. Of course implementation of such a plan in wartime was impossible. During 1940, German authorities settled on the temporary solution of ghettoization. All Jews were to be isolated and concentrated in specifically designated areas. There they would await the next step—whatever it might be.

In April 1940, Nazis established the first major ghetto in the Polish city of Lodz. Soon Jews all over Poland were being forced to relocate. Gypsies were dumped in the ghettos as well, at least 5,000 of them in Lodz and 10,000 in Warsaw. The Germans intended the ghettos to be self-supporting, but they sealed them off and provided no resources for the people inside. They called the ghettos self-administering, but the Jewish Councils they established had little freedom of action except to carry out German orders. If Jewish leaders refused to cooperate, the Germans shot them and forced others to take their places.

All of the ghettos were painfully overcrowded, with as many as seven people living in each small room. In Lodz, as in most cities, the ghetto was located in the worst section of the city. It included about 30,000 apartments, most of them one-room, and only 725 with running water. As many as 200,000 people tried somehow to live there. Starvation and disease—typhus, pneumonia, tuberculosis, influenza, and dysentery—ran rampant. Periodically the Germans swept through, rounding people up for forced labor. Death tolls skyrocketed. In 1940, 6,000 people perished in the Lodz ghetto. The following year the number almost doubled to 11,000. By 1942, it reached 18,000. "Walk a hundred yards in the ghetto," a survivor named Simon Srebnik recalls, "and there would be two hundred bodies" (Lanzmann, video 1).

Stanislav Rozycki, a visitor to the Warsaw ghetto, described children dying of hunger in the streets: "They howl, beg, sing, moan, shiver with cold, without underwear, without clothing, without shoes, in rags, sacks, flannel which are bound in strips round the emaciated skeletons, children swollen with hunger, disfigured, half conscious, already completely grown-up at the age of five, gloomy and weary of life" (Noakes and Pridham, II: p. 1067). Sometimes Nazis organized bus tours through the ghettos. Pointing to the disastrous conditions, they claimed to find proof that Jews were indeed subhuman.

The Decision for Mass Murder

In June 1941, German troops violated the nonaggression pact and invaded the Soviet Union. From the beginning of this new phase of the war, it was clear that the Germans intended to proceed with unprecedented ruthlessness against the five million Soviet Jews as well as high-ranking communists and Slavic civilians who offered resistance. Sometime during 1941, Hitler and his inner circle crossed the line from persecution and assault of Jews to systematic efforts at annihilation.

Nazi authorities set up special murder squads to follow the regular military into Soviet territory. Those units, called the *Einsatzgruppen,* consisted of between 500 and 1,000 men each, many of them highly educated: lawyers, theologians, and other professionals. Their task was to kill prominent communists and anyone suspected of sabotage or anti-German activity. Very soon they began interpreting their job as the extermination of all Jews including women and children. The *Einsatzgruppen* also murdered Gypsies and inmates of mental hospitals. Standard practice was to dig pits, force the victims to undress, and then shoot groups of them directly into the graves. In that way, in just two days in September 1941, Germans killed about 35,000 Jews and an unknown number of other people at Babi Yar, a ravine outside of the Ukrainian city of Kiev. Altogether, the Germans and their henchmen slaughtered about one and a half million Jews in open-air shootings, even before the construction of death camps and gas chambers.

Often the Nazis staged their attacks on Jewish holidays. On Rosh Hashannah 1941, the Jewish new year, Germans and their local helpers liquidated the Jewish population of a Lithuanian town called Eisysky. A young boy named Zvi Michalowsky was among those forced to strip and await a bullet at the edge of a grave. Zvi threw himself into the pit a split second before the Germans fired. Miraculously, he avoided serious injury. For the rest of the day he lay in the grave, feeling the bodies piling up on top of him. Only long after the shooting had stopped did he dare to climb out. He ran, naked and covered with blood, to the nearest house. But when he knocked, the terrified Polish Christians refused to let him in. Finally he approached an old woman. He told her he was Jesus Christ come down from the cross. She opened the door. Zvi Michalowsky, one of the few people to survive an *Einsatzgruppen* massacre, went on to found a Jewish resistance group in the woods of Lithuania (Eliach, pp. 53–55).

The Death Camps

By the end of 1941, Nazi authorities concluded that mass shootings were not the most efficient way to execute the Final Solution. Their concerns were not with the victims but rather with the perpetrators, who found it psychologically difficult to kill all day long at close range. On 20 January 1942, representatives from the key agencies involved in genocide—the military, Nazi party, SS, *Einsatzgruppen,* foreign ministry, and others—met to try to streamline their efforts. That meeting, known as the Wannsee Conference, marks a turning point in the killing process. Mass murder was already under way, but at the Wannsee Conference, the SS asserted its leadership in the extermination of the Jews. Death camps equipped with gas chambers emerged as the killing method of choice.

One death camp, at Chelmno, had already begun operations in December 1941, even before the Wannsee Conference met. Within months of the conference, five more camps had been equipped with gas chambers, all of them, like Chelmno, in territories that had once belonged to Poland. These six death camps allowed the Nazis to achieve unprecedented levels of killing.

The camps differed in many ways. Some of them, like Sobibor and Treblinka, were exclusively for killing, and the only prisoners kept alive beyond arrival were the handful needed to run the operation and perform the dirty work—disposing of corpses, cleaning wastes— that the Germans refused to do. Other camps, like Belzec, Majdanek, and Auschwitz-Birkenau, included slave labor sections as well as facilities for mass killing. Methods of killing differed as well. At Chelmno, the Germans used specially equipped vans in which the exhaust was piped into the rear compartment. Drivers proceeded slowly for two and a half miles from the collection point into the woods. In that time, fumes asphyxiated the passengers. Their bodies were dumped, a work crew buried or burned them, and the van returned for another load. On a "normal" day of twelve or thirteen trips, about 1,000 Jews were killed this way. Belzec was the site of experimentation with diesel fumes, while Zyklon B was first used at Auschwitz-Birkenau.

The horrors of the camps are almost impossible to imagine. One man, assigned to a work unit at Chelmno, found the bodies of his wife and two children in the forest. He begged the SS guards to shoot him. When they refused, he tried to commit suicide. This time his comrades stopped him. Eventually he escaped. One of very few survivors of that camp, he later served as a central witness at the postwar Chelmno trial.

Altogether the Germans killed more than three million Jews in the six death camps. They gassed Gypsies as well, at Chelmno and Auschwitz-Birkenau, for example. Members of other target groups—homosexuals, Jehovah's Witnesses, communists, Polish intellectuals, prisoners of war—experienced the deprivation and brutality of the camps, too. But, with very few exceptions, they were not sent to the gas.

Nazi camps were a bizarre world of distortion and brutality. Freight trains generally brought the prisoners to the site. In order to maintain calm, Nazi authorities deceived them as to the real purpose of the camp for as long as possible. Such deception made the Germans' murderous jobs easier, too. Commandant Franz Stangl at Sobibor and Treblinka had flowers planted to beautify the arrival site. Himmler ordered the construction of fish farms and gardens at some of the camps. Respected doctors like Josef Mengele set up laboratories where they used their "disposable" human subjects for deadly experiments. Still, it was impossible to conceal the stench that hung in the air for miles around the camps: the smell of burning human bodies. Polish farmers tended their fields right up to the fence, and local women worked as typists inside. The camps, like the murder of the handicapped, the ghettos, and the open-air shootings, could not be kept secret.

Most of the Jews brought to death camps—children, the young, elderly, sick or weak, pregnant women, and mothers accompanying children—were sent immediately to the gas. Those kept alive endured bone-crushing labor, disease, starvation, and abuse by guards and even fellow prisoners. Accounts by young Jewish women in the camps often emphasize the physical transformation that they underwent. Isabella Leitner, a survivor from Hungary, described her feelings in Auschwitz in May 1944:

> Our heads are shaved. We look like neither boys nor girls. We haven't menstruated for a long time. We have diarrhea. No, not diarrhea—typhus. Summer and winter we have but one type of clothing. Its name is "rag." Not an inch of it without a hole. Our shoulders are exposed. The rain is pouring on our skeletal bodies. The lice are having an orgy in our armpits, their favorite spots. Their bloodsucking, the irritation, their busy scurrying give the illusion of warmth. We're hot at least under our armpits, while our bodies are shivering (Rittner and Roth, p. 67).

Many accounts from the camps stress the importance of networks of support between prisoners. The Nazis devised the camp system to divide and conquer their prey. They set people against each other by forcing competition for absurdly small prizes—an extra crust of bread, a button, a piece of string. Some of the most powerful stories of the Holocaust explain how inmates in the camps countered such efforts to dehumanize and isolate them. The Italian Jew Primo Levi tells how he reminded himself and a co-worker of their human dignity by reciting lines from Dante's *Divine Comedy:* "Think of your breed; for brutish ignorance/Your mettle was not made; you were made men,/To follow after knowledge and excellence" (Levi, p. 103). Sara Nomberg-Przytyk, a Polish Jewish woman, attributes her survival to an anonymous woman in the next traincar who sacrificed her own blanket so that Sara would not freeze to death (Nomberg

Przytyk, pp. 132–36). Ruth Klüger, a Viennese Jew who arrived at the so-called family camp in Auschwitz-Birkenau when she was twelve, describes how a fellow prisoner saved her from the gas. An SS man had "selected" her for death, but his clerk, a prisoner herself, urged him to reconsider. Look at her muscular calves, the clerk insisted. That girl can work. The SS man agreed to send Ruth and her mother to a labor camp. They survived. Like every story of life in the Holocaust, Ruth Klüger's account is set against a backdrop of death and destruction. All remaining inmates of the family camp, she tells us in her memoir, were gassed in July 1944 (Klüger, p. 132–33).

The Issue of Resistance

Not all of those targeted for killing in the Holocaust ended up in death camps. Many Jews fled, taking refuge where they could. In the summer of 1939, about 17,000 Jews from Germany and Austria were shipped to Shanghai where they lived out the war. Others hid, and still others "passed" as gentiles. An estimated 80,000 to 120,000 Jews were hidden in Poland; maybe half of those survived the war. All across Nazi-occupied Europe, Jews and other opponents of Nazism took to the woods, often forming partisan units to combat the Germans.

Little is known about the precarious existence of Jewish partisans. They lived from hand to mouth, stealing when necessary, arranging secretly for deliveries of food, spending hours and even days in holes in the ground when danger threatened. Afraid that the presence of Jews nearby would jeopardize their own security, gentiles often denounced or killed their Jewish counterparts. Nevertheless, as German police records for 1943 and 1944 indicate, Jews in the woods managed to acquire explosives and weapons and to perform acts of sabotage against the Germans. From Jewish sources we know that in at least one case, a young man and woman also married in the woods and gave birth to a child. Such commitment to hope was itself a powerful act of resistance.

Jewish resistance of various kinds was much more widespread than historians used to assume. In Lithuania in early 1942, about 10,000 Jewish women and men were fighting as partisans. At least thirty different Jewish partisan groups existed in the *Generalgouvernement* alone. Jews also revolted in major ghettos such as Warsaw and Bialystok, and violent incidents occurred in many smaller towns. In general, the groups that banded together were desperate, pitifully small, and barely armed. Their chances of success were minimal, but still they defied Nazi power.

Even in the camps, under the most adverse conditions, resistance in many forms occurred. Numerous survivors' memoirs tell the story of the beautiful dancer in Auschwitz who seized a gun from an SS-man and shot him. In May 1943, the Germans planned to "liquidate" the Gypsy family camp in Auschwitz-Birkenau. Gypsy prisoners fought back. They were unable to turn the tide, but they did force the SS to postpone their final assault. Both Sobibor and Treblinka witnessed revolts in 1943 that resulted in some escapes and probably also contributed to the closing of those camps later that year. In October 1944, Jewish prisoners at Auschwitz-Birkenau blew up the camp's fourth crematorium. Starved, abandoned by the world, and robbed of all their property, the Jews were in the weakest imaginable position to offer resistance to the Germans. Nevertheless, they did resist—violently, passively, spiritually, physically, and emotionally—throughout the entire process of the Final Solution.

The End of the War

As Allied troops moved into German-held territory in the last months of the war, they encountered shocking scenes. Soldiers from the United States and Great Britain in particular were unprepared for the mass graves, abandoned camps, boxcars full of corpses, and emaciated, dying prisoners that they found. On 15 April 1945, the first British tanks entered the concentration camp of Bergen-Belsen. Terrorized and enfeebled, inmates of the camp could not believe they were free. And in fact, freedom did not come easily. After initial contact, the British tanks moved on. For the next forty-eight hours, the camp was only nominally under British control. Fifteen hundred Hungarian soldiers who had been stationed there as guards remained in command. In those two days, they shot seventy-two Jews and eleven non-Jews, for offenses like taking potato peels from the kitchen. And even after British troops entered Belsen in force, for more than two weeks 300 inmates continued to die daily of typhus and starvation. Horror on the scale of the Holocaust did not simply disappear with the arrival of the Allied "liberators."

On 15 April 1945, the same day that the British reached Belsen, SS and camp guards forced 17,000 women and 40,000 men to march westward from the concentration camps of Ravensbrück and Sachsenhausen into territories still in German hands. As the Allies closed in, German authorities tried to empty out the camps and relocate prisoners. The resulting forced treks have become known as death marches. Whole columns of prisoners stumbled ahead, driven on by SS supervisors and their dogs. Hundreds of women died of exhaustion on the march from the women's camp at Ravensbrück that April. Retreating guards and SS men shot hundreds of others. Some were even killed by Allied bombs. Having made it so long, thousands died by the roadside just days away from the end of the war. For them liberation came too late.

Even for those who lived, the end of the war brought the realization of all that had been destroyed. Alone, without family, friends, or home, many survivors had nowhere to go. Those who did try to reclaim properties and possessions often encountered hostility from their former neighbors. Polish Jews who returned "home" often met with violence and even death. True liberation, the surviving targets of Nazi aggression would discover, was impossible in a hostile society. Many Jewish survivors accordingly turned their backs on Europe and started new lives in the United States and Israel.

References

Eliach, Yaffa. 1982. *Hasidic Tales of the Holocaust.* New York: Vintage Books.

Jäckel, Eberhard. 1981. *Hitler's World View: A Blueprint for Power.* Cambridge, Massachusetts: Harvard University Press.

Klüger, Ruth. 1992. *Weiter leben.* Göttingen: Wallstein Verlag.

Lanzmann, Claude. 1985. *Shoah.* 5 videoscassettes. France.

Levi, Primo. 1978. *Survival in Auschwitz.* New York: Collier Books.

Noakes, Jeremy, and Geoffrey Pridham (eds.). 1988. *Nazism: A History in Documents and Eyewitness Accounts, 1919–1945.* 2 vols. New York: Schocken Books.

Nomberg-Przytyk, Sara. 1985. *Auschwitz: True Tales from a Grotesque Land.* Trans. Roslyn Hirsch. Chapel Hill, North Carolina: University of North Carolina Press.

Rittner, Carol and John K. Roth, (eds.). 1993. *Different Voices: Women and the Holocaust.* New York: Paragon.

Stabholz, Thaddeus. 1990. *Seven Hells.* Trans. Jacques and Hilda R. Grunblatt. New York: Holocaust Library.

Genocide at the Cambodian Killing Fields

Doug Bandow

From April 1975 to January 1979, the small Southeast Asian country of Cambodia was ruled by the Khmer Rouge, a communist organization led by Pol Pot. Of the nation's eight million people, between one and two million perished during this time from starvation or in massacres perpetrated by the ruling regime. In the following article, Doug Bandow recounts the terrible details of the genocide in the course of describing his visit to several memorials in Cambodia a quarter century later. The Khmer Rouge began by eliminating its political opponents, he writes, but eventually the killing spread to entire classes of people. Bandow is a nationally syndicated columnist and the author of several books, including *Tripwire: Korea and U.S. Foreign Policy in a Changed World.*

Phnom Penh, Cambodia—The white monument juts up 40 feet or so, dominating the surrounding fields and trees. From a distance it looks like it could commemorate most anything—a military victory, important statesman, or historical event. But this monument is different. It is filled with skulls.

On April 17, 1975, Phnom Penh fell to the Khmer Rouge. As in Vietnam, an American-backed regime—corrupt, undemocratic, leaderless—collapsed in the face of determined nationalistic communists. In Vietnam the result was repression and poverty. In Cambodia it was slaughter.

The Khmer Rouge, led by Brother Number One, or Pol Pot, summarily executed leaders of the old regime, emptied the cities, forced everyone into communes, and launched social engineering on a vast scale. Before being ousted by a Vietnamese invasion less than four years later, the Khmer Rouge had killed as many as two million people, an astonishing one-quarter of the population.

The number numbs. Hitler, Stalin, and Mao each murdered more people. But none managed to slaughter one-quarter of his nation's population.

Reprinted from Doug Bandow, "Visiting the Killing Fields," *Ideas on Liberty,* August 2000. Reprinted with permission from *Ideas on Liberty.*

Pol Pot's reign of terror filled the country. Some regions, particularly Ratanakiri province, the home base of the Khmer Rouge, suffered less than others. But four in ten residents of Phnom Penh are thought to have died.

Yet mass murder seems more a statistic than a tragedy. A thousand, a million. What do such numbers mean without individual victims?

The Killing Fields

Those victims are evident at Choeung Ek, known simply as the Killing Fields. Fifteen kilometers outside of Phnom Penh—down a country road, past shacks and homes, next to a school—are the grounds in which some 20,000 people were buried.

Only 86 of 129 mass graves have been excavated. The 86 have yielded 8,985 victims, whose skulls and bones are stored in the 17-level monument. Atop the large holes are signs listing the number of bodies—450 in one about 20 feet long by ten wide, for instance. "Many holes, same, same," explained my guide.

But there's more. Stub your toe on the path in between holes and you're not likely to find stones. It is more likely the tip of a leg bone or a jaw poking through the dirt.

The Khmer Rouge didn't just murder. They did so as painfully as possible, using axes, poles, hammers, and knives. Babies were simply swung against a tree. No one was immune from revolutionary "justice."

However, Choeung Ek was the end, not the beginning. Most of those buried here started in Phnom Penh, at Tuol Sleng prison.

Tuol Sleng

Tuol Sleng sits in an area scarcely bigger than a football field and began life as a high school. But in May 1976 the Khmer Rouge established Security Office 21, or S-21. Its purpose was to expose and exterminate enemies of the regime.

Choeung Ek brutally overwhelms through its pile of skulls. Tuol Sleng is even more powerful. It features photos of the living as well as of the dead.

The Khmer Rouge were nothing if not meticulous. They kept arrest and execution records and filed confessions; they also numbered and photographed incoming prisoners, often in profile as well as in front.

It is the images of the living that haunt. Men and women. Boys and girls. Babies. The photos line the walls. Four roomfuls. Faces of people. Once alive. Now dead.

A few look defiant, smoldering hatred evident in their eyes. Others look bewildered. Many radiate fear, eyes wide at the fate they knew to be before them. One seemed to be crying, almost begging for his life.

But most look dead. Their hearts beat, blood flowed, and nerves transmitted pain, but their eyes were lifeless. Empty. Their humanity had been wrung out of them and casually tossed aside.

One picture is particularly unnerving. A man sporting the number 162 sits with a vacant stare. He knows only too well that his life will soon be over.

Tuol Sleng was, first and foremost, an interrogation center. Khmer Rouge interrogation meant torture. And torture often meant death.

Tools of Death and Torture

The tools are all on display. The metal bed frames and wooden slab to which inmates were shackled, then beaten. The metal and wooden tubs in which people were drowned. The high bar from which inmates were dangled. The boxes that housed the scorpions that were set on prisoners. The electrical wires with which shocks were administered. And the clubs, axes, hammers, shovels, and knives used to punish and kill.

Although death was the ultimate end, the Khmer Rouge thoughtfully strung barbed wire around the cellblocks to prevent prisoners from committing suicide. You would die, but only when the party thought the time was right.

And that time was only after you confessed. As Martin Stuard-Fox and Bunheang Ung explain in their book, *Murderous Revolution,* enemies "were never simply arrested and shot: authorities had first to obtain confessions which would justify their arrest, and thus confirm the omniscience and justice of Angkar [the Communist Party] in arresting them."

If there was any justice at Tuol Sleng, it was that Khmer Rouge cadre were among the victims. This revolution, like so many revolutions before it, consumed its own.

These memorials in Phnom Penh reflect only the small tip of a pervasive system of murder. Reports French scholar Henri Locard, "From 17th April, the entire country was to become in a way one big prison."

Three Waves of Killing

There were three waves of imprisonments and murders. The first was directed against almost anyone associated with the fallen Lon Nol regime. In general, the victims were murdered outside of any formal prison.

The second bout of repression began in the latter part of 1975 and was directed against the same classes of people, including professionals and civil servants. Many of these victims had either been denounced by enemies or prisoners, or had revealed incriminating details of their pasts when writing their autobiographies for the new rulers. These arrests coincided with establishment of a national prison network.

The final round of brutality began in 1976 and, explains Locard, "swept through all classes of the new society," including "the Khmer Rouge cadres and military personnel themselves. All categories of the revolutionary society were soon engulfed in the maelstrom of repression as the regime was getting more and more deranged and saw 'enemies,' khmang, everywhere." Even at the information and foreign ministries in Phnom Penh.

But most of Cambodia's dead, at Choeung Ek and elsewhere, were innocent—the victims of totalitarian egalitarianism, in which life means nothing and the collective means everything. Alas, the world is full of monuments to incredible evil cloaked with the rhetoric of humanity. Few are more moving than Cambodia's Killing Fields.

ETHNIC CLEANSING IN BOSNIA-HERZEGOVINA

Philip Gavin

A recent incident of genocide, according to many observers, took place in the small country of Bosnia-Herzegovina during the 1990s. Following Bosnia's declaration of independence from Yugoslavia in 1992, a three-year war broke out among the country's Serbian, Croatian, and Muslim ethnic groups. The following overview of the conflict by Philip Gavin describes Serbian violence against both Croats and Muslims during the war, including mass shootings and the use of concentration camps. The international media used the term "ethnic cleansing" to describe the Serbian actions, which struck many outside observers as genocidal and chillingly reminiscent of German proceedings against the Jews during World War II. Gavin is the publisher of the History Place, an award-winning internet publication for history students.

In the Republic of Bosnia-Herzegovina, conflict between the three main ethnic groups, the Serbs, Croats, and Muslims, resulted in genocide committed by the Serbs against the Muslims in Bosnia.

Bosnia is one of several small countries that emerged from the breakup of Yugoslavia, a multicultural country created after World War I by the victorious Western Allies. Yugoslavia was composed of ethnic and religious groups that had been historical rivals, even bitter enemies, including the Serbs (Orthodox Christians), Croats (Catholics), and ethnic Albanians (Muslims).

During World War II, Yugoslavia was invaded by Nazi Germany and was partitioned. A fierce resistance movement sprang up led by Josip Tito. Following Germany's defeat, Tito reunified Yugoslavia under the slogan "Brotherhood and Unity," merging together Slovenia, Croatia, Bosnia, Serbia, Montenegro, Macedonia, along with two self-governing provinces, Kosovo and Vojvodina.

Tito, a Communist, was a strong leader who maintained ties with the Soviet Union and the United States during the Cold War, playing one superpower against the other while obtaining financial assistance and other aid from both. After his death in 1980 and without his

Reprinted from Philip Gavin, "Genocide in the 20th Century: Bosnia-Herzegovina 1992-1995," available at www.historyplace.com/worldhistory/genocide/bosnia.htm. Reprinted with permission from the author.

39

strong leadership, Yugoslavia quickly plunged into political and economic chaos.

A new leader arose by the late 1980s, a Serbian named Slobodan
Milosevic, a former Communist who had turned to nationalism and
religious hatred to gain power. He began by inflaming long-standing
tensions between Serbs and Muslims in the independent province of
Kosovo. Orthodox Christian Serbs in Kosovo were in the minority
and claimed they were being mistreated by the Albanian Muslim
majority. Serbian-backed political unrest in Kosovo eventually led to
its loss of independence and domination by Milosevic.

In June 1991, Slovenia and Croatia both declared their independence from Yugoslavia, soon resulting in civil war. The national army
of Yugoslavia, now made up of Serbs controlled by Milosevic, stormed
into Slovenia but failed to subdue the separatists there and withdrew
after only ten days of fighting.

Conflict in Croatia

Milosevic quickly lost interest in Slovenia, a country with almost no
Serbs. Instead, he turned his attention to Croatia, a Catholic country
where Orthodox Serbs made up 12 percent of the population.

During World War II, Croatia had been a pro-Nazi state led by Ante
Pavelic and his fascist Ustasha Party. Serbs living in Croatia as well as
Jews had been the targets of widespread Ustasha massacres. In the
concentration camp at Jasenovac, they had been slaughtered by the
tens of thousands.

In 1991, the new Croat government, led by Franjo Tudjman,
seemed to be reviving fascism, even using the old Ustasha flag, and
also enacted discriminatory laws targeting Orthodox Serbs.

Aided by Serbian guerilla in Croatia, Milosevic's forces invaded in
July 1991 to 'protect' the Serbian minority. In the city of Vukovar,
they bombarded the outgunned Croats for eighty six consecutive days
and reduced it to rubble. After Vukovar fell, the Serbs began the first
mass executions of the conflict, killing hundreds of Croat men and
burying them in mass graves.

The response of the international community was limited. The United States under President George Bush chose not to get involved militarily, but instead recognized the independence of both Slovenia and Croatia. An arms embargo was imposed for all of the former Yugoslavia by
the United Nations. However, the Serbs under Milosevic were already
the best armed force and thus maintained a big military advantage.

By the end of 1991, a U.S.–sponsored cease-fire agreement was bro-
kered between the Serbs and Croats fighting in Croatia.

War in Bosnia

In April 1992, the United States and European Community chose to
recognize the independence of Bosnia, a mostly Muslim country

where the Serb minority made up 32 percent of the population. Milosevic responded to Bosnia's declaration of independence by attacking Sarajevo, its capital city, best known for hosting the 1984 Winter Olympics. Sarajevo soon became known as the city where Serb snipers continually shot down helpless civilians in the streets, including eventually over 3,500 children.

Bosnian Muslims were hopelessly outgunned. As the Serbs gained ground, they began to systematically round up local Muslims in scenes eerily similar to those that had occurred under the Nazis during World War II, including mass shootings, forced repopulation of entire towns, and confinement in makeshift concentration camps for men and boys. The Serbs also terrorized Muslim families into fleeing their villages by using rape as a weapon against women and girls.

The actions of the Serbs were labeled as 'ethnic cleansing,' a name which quickly took hold among the international media.

Despite media reports of the secret camps, the mass killings, as well as the destruction of Muslim mosques and historic architecture in Bosnia, the world community remained mostly indifferent. The United Nations (U.N.) responded by imposing economic sanctions on Serbia and also deployed its troops to protect the distribution of food and medicine to dispossessed Muslims. But the U.N. strictly prohibited its troops from interfering militarily against the Serbs. Thus they remained steadfastly neutral no matter how bad the situation became.

Throughout 1993, confident that the U.N., United States, and the European Community would not take military action, Serbs in Bosnia freely committed genocide against Muslims. Bosnian Serbs operated under the local leadership of Radovan Karadzic, president of the illegitimate Bosnian Serb Republic. Karadzic had once told a group of journalists, "Serbs and Muslims are like cats and dogs. They cannot live together in peace. It is impossible."

When Karadzic was confronted by reporters about ongoing atrocities, he bluntly denied involvement of his soldiers or special police units.

On February 6, 1994, the world's attention turned completely to Bosnia as a marketplace in Sarajevo was struck by a Serb mortar shell, killing 68 persons and wounding nearly 200. Sights and sounds of the bloody carnage were broadcast globally by the international news media and soon resulted in calls for military intervention against the Serbs.

NATO Involvement

The United States under its new President, Bill Clinton, who had promised during his election campaign in 1992 to stop the ethnic cleansing in Bosnia, now issued an ultimatum through the North Atlantic Treaty Organization (NATO) demanding that the Serbs withdraw their artillery from Sarajevo. The Serbs quickly complied and a NATO-imposed cease-fire in Sarajevo was declared.

The United States then launched diplomatic efforts aimed at unifying Bosnian Muslims and the Croats against the Serbs. However, this new Muslim-Croat alliance failed to stop the Serbs from attacking Muslim towns in Bosnia, which had been declared Safe Havens by the U.N. A total of six Muslim towns had been established as Safe Havens in May 1993 under the supervision of U.N. peacekeepers.

Bosnian Serbs not only attacked the Safe Havens but also attacked the U.N. peacekeepers as well. NATO forces responded by launching limited air strikes against Serb ground positions. The Serbs retaliated by taking hundreds of U.N. peacekeepers as hostages and turning them into human shields, chained to military targets such as ammo supply dumps.

At this point, some of the worst genocidal activities of the four-year-old conflict occurred. In Srebrenica, a Safe Haven, U.N. peacekeepers stood by helplessly as the Serbs under the command of General Ratko Mladic systematically selected and then slaughtered nearly 8,000 men and boys between the ages of twelve and sixty—the worst mass murder in Europe since World War II. In addition, the Serbs continued to engage in mass rapes of Muslim females.

On August 30, 1995, effective military intervention finally began as the United States led a massive NATO bombing campaign in response to the killings at Srebrenica, targeting Serbian artillery positions throughout Bosnia. The bombardment continued into October. Serb forces also lost ground to Bosnian Muslims who had received arms shipments from the Islamic world. As a result, half of Bosnia was eventually retaken by Muslim-Croat troops.

Faced with the heavy NATO bombardment and a string of ground losses to the Muslim-Croat alliance, Serb leader Milosevic was now ready to talk peace. On November 1, 1995, leaders of the warring factions including Milosevic and Tudjman traveled to the United States for peace talks at Wright-Patterson Air Force base in Ohio.

After three weeks of negotiations, a peace accord was declared. Terms of the agreement included partitioning Bosnia into two main portions known as the Bosnian Serb Republic and the Muslim-Croat Federation. The agreement also called for democratic elections and stipulated that war criminals would be handed over for prosecution. Sixty thousand NATO soldiers were deployed to preserve the cease-fire.

By now, over 200,000 Muslim civilians had been systematically murdered. More than 20,000 were missing and feared dead, while 2,000,000 had become refugees. It was, according to U.S. Assistant Secretary of State Richard Holbrooke, "the greatest failure of the West since the 1930s."

GENOCIDE IN RWANDA

Stephen R. Shalom

The African country of Rwanda is divided between the Hutu and Tutsi ethnic groups. In April 1994, the Hutu-dominated Rwandan government and military began an organized campaign to kill Tutsis; hundreds of thousands were slain before Tutsi-led rebels overthrew the government in July. In the following article, Stephen R. Shalom provides a general overview of the Rwandan genocide and the historical background that led to the events of 1994. Furthermore, he argues that the international community could have done much more than it did to prevent the Rwandan atrocities. Shalom teaches political science at William Paterson University in New Jersey. His books include *Imperial Alibis: Rationalizing U.S. Intervention After the Cold War* and *Socialist Visions*.

For 100 horrendous days in 1994, genocide took place in the small African country of Rwanda. The term "genocide" has been used with varying degrees of precision, but even under the most demanding definition there is no doubt that the events in Rwanda between April and July 1994 qualified as genocide.

Members of the Tutsi ethnic group, who made up about 14 percent of Rwanda's eight million people, were targeted for extermination. The victims were all unarmed civilians. Neither age nor gender nor infirmity were protection against the killers. Those who sought refuge in churches, hospitals, or schools were butchered just the same. The killers were not content to merely expel the Tutsis from Rwanda; Tutsis had been allowed to leave in 1959, the genocide's ideologues declared, but the same mistake would not be made again. The number of Tutsi dead may never be known, but serious estimates place the toll at between half a million and a million. Gérard Prunier, in his valuable *The Rwanda Crisis: History of A Genocide* (Columbia University Press), puts Tutsi deaths at 800,000.

The killers were all from Rwanda's majority Hutu ethnic group, but the extremists who orchestrated the massacres went after Hutus as well, eliminating politicians, human rights activists, journalists, and any other moderate Hutu thought to stand in the way of the genocidal

Excerpted from Stephen R. Shalom, "The Rwanda Genocide," *Z Magazine*, April, 1996. Reprinted with permission from the author.

project. Prunier estimates that some 10,000–30,000 moderate Hutus were slaughtered.

The killers and their victims were all Rwandans. The genocide, however, cannot be understood without grasping the crucial role played by outsiders.

The Colonial Legacy

In precolonial Rwanda, the categories "Tutsi" and "Hutu" were somewhere between castes and ethnic groups. The boundaries between the two groups were permeable, with movement permitted between them. Some members of each group were local chiefs and there was no systematic Tutsi-Hutu violence. The brief period of German colonial rule brought European racial theories to Rwanda: the more European-featured Tutsis were deemed to be the natural-born local rulers and the Hutus destined to serve them. These theories were put into practice by the Belgians who took over from the Germans after World War I. They replaced existing Hutu chiefs with Tutsis and issued identity cards indicating each person's ethnic group, thus eliminating some of the social mobility of the old system.

The Rwandan state was always highly centralized—a function of the country's extremely dense population—but became even more centralized under Belgian rule, and life for the average Rwandan became even more oppressive. Forced labor was made more onerous, taxes were increased, and beatings became standard. A United Nations (UN) mission in 1948 found that of 250 peasants interviewed, 247 had been beaten.

In the 1950s, elite Tutsis began agitating for independence, and the Belgians began to shift their support to the Hutu elite, who would likely be easier to control since they lacked the experience of domination. Communist governments at the UN championed the cause of Rwandan independence, further straining relations between Belgians and Tutsis. In 1959, ethnic clashes broke out, and the Belgians allowed Hutus to burn down Tutsi houses without intervening. Two weeks later, there were 300 dead and most of those arrested by the Belgians were Tutsi.

Starting in 1960, the Belgians replaced most Tutsi chiefs with Hutus, who proceeded to organize persecution of Tutsis. The UN tried to promote some form of reconciliation, but the Belgians, to forestall any further UN interference, arranged in 1961 for the Hutu elite to engineer a legal coup and declare its independence. The Hutu elite claimed they represented democratic majority rule, but they were establishing a racialist state, seeking to maintain their control over the impoverished Hutu population by portraying the Tutsis as a well-off, alien minority, just as European elites had earlier used anti-Semitism. The UN Trusteeship Commission reported with much accuracy that an "oppressive system has been replaced by another one."

Anti-Tutsi violence continued, driving many Tutsis into exile, some of whom organized raids back into Rwanda. After a major exile raid was repulsed in December 1963, some 10,000 Tutsis were slaughtered over the next two months. By the end of 1964, there were 336,000 Tutsi refugees. Some integrated themselves into neighboring societies, but others hoped to return to Rwanda. In Rwanda, ethnic quotas were established to limit Tutsi participation in schools, the civil service, and other government employment, and refugees were denied any right of return.

Neighboring Burundi shared Rwanda's colonial background and ethnic makeup. However, the Tutsi elite there, seeing where "democratization" had led in Rwanda, had ruthlessly held on to power by controlling the army. In 1972, after a failed uprising by some Hutus, the Tutsi leaders responded by massacring any educated Hutus. Four months later, conservative estimates put the death toll at 80,000–100,000 in a nation of 3.5 million. Among themselves, U.S. officials characterized what was going on at the time in Burundi as "selective genocide," but Washington issued no public criticism, made no private remonstrance, and did not use its leverage over the Burundian economy to force an end to the killing.

In Rwanda, the Hutu ruler tried to use the Burundian massacres as an excuse for anti-Tutsi actions, hoping that the popular mobilization might bolster his faltering regime. A few dozen Tutsis were killed, propelling more into exile, but the Hutu elite split and in July 1973 Major-General Juvénal Habyarimana (a Hutu) took over in a bloodless coup.

The Habyarimana Regime

Under Habyarimana discrimination against Tutsis continued, but as long as they didn't get involved in politics they were generally left in peace, and there were no ethnic massacres between 1973–90. Habyarimana, however, was a dictator and he established one party rule. His National Revolutionary Movement for Development (MRND) was, in Prunier's words, "a truly totalitarian party"; administrative control under Habyarimana "was probably the tightest in the world among non-communist countries." . . .

In June 1990, French President François Mitterrand called for multiparty systems in Africa (a position from which he was soon to retreat). Back in 1975, Paris had signed a military cooperation and training agreement with (the Habyarimana regime in) Kigali (Rwanda's capital), and France had gradually replaced Belgium as the dominant power in Rwanda. A month after Mitterrand's comments, Habyarimana declared that he agreed with the French position. Despite his insincerity, the country's democratic opposition—Hutu and Tutsi—pressed for a multiparty system and democratic reforms. . . .

Civil War

In October 1990, the Rwandan Patriotic Front (RPF), an organization of primarily Tutsi refugees from Uganda, invaded the country to obtain the right to return to Rwanda and to overthrow the dictatorial Habyarimana regime. Many of the RPF soldiers were veterans of civil war in Uganda, where they had fought for a nonethnically based regime, some rising to high positions in the Ugandan military. In 1987, the Tutsi refugees formed the RPF with the intention of establishing a nonethnic state in Rwanda. A few Hutu Rwandans joined the RPF, but it remained largely a Tutsi organization; it had a progressive ideology, though some of its members were Tutsi supremacists.

Prunier suggests that the Ugandan president likely knew the general outline of the RPF invasion plan and didn't try to stop it, but certainly wasn't behind it. The Ugandan leader assumed Habyarimana also knew about the invasion, the threat of which would make him more willing to negotiate on the refugee question. In fact, argues Prunier, Habyarimana knew about the coming invasion and was determined to use it to crush his internal opposition.

Belgium and France sent troops to Rwanda to evacuate their nationals from the country. Belgium withdrew its forces promptly and cut off military aid in a situation of civil war. French troops, however, stayed on. To Paris, Africa was the one place where the glory of the French empire could still live on. "Without Africa," Mitterrand had written in 1957, "France will have no history in the 21st century." Prime Minister Edouard Balladur explained that "France sees itself as a world power. This is its ambition and its honor." And its "main field of action is Africa," especially French-speaking Africa. But it was not just a matter of honor. Corrupt African rulers helped finance French political parties, aided with money laundering, provided sweetheart deals to well-connected French companies, and voted with Paris at the UN. And Mitterrand's son was then head of the Africa Office at the Elysée [Foreign Ministry] and personally close to the Habyarimana family.

Habyarimana arrested almost 10,000 of his political opponents, while some 350 Tutsi civilians were massacred in the countryside, the killers acting under the authority of local officials. In early 1991, further massacres were carried out. The Rwandan army grew tenfold from October 1990 to mid-1992, and France provided all the weapons, either directly or by secretly arranging foreign arms contracts from Egypt or South Africa. The Rwandan government gave a French military officer overall command of counterinsurgency operations, and the French staffed roadblocks, fired artillery, and served as advisers to Rwandan field commanders. . . .

Habyarimana's repression, however, did not intimidate the democratic opposition. In January 1992, 50,000 people marched in a prodemocracy demonstration in Kigali. Some members of Habyarimana's inner circle favored violence on a massive scale to crush the opposition, but for the moment Habyarimana agreed to form a coalition cabinet. Members of the opposition parties took over a number of cabinet positions, including that of prime minister. Habyarimana, however, was by no means conceding defeat. His party remained the largest in the government, controlling the Defense and Interior portfolios among others. Death squads were set up within the military. MRND civil servants countermanded instructions from opposition ministers. In March 1992, the Habyarimana clique employed a new tactic, foreshadowing the genocide to come: the interahamwe, the MRND's "youth group"—but actually a militia organization, trained, armed, and indoctrinated in racial hatred by the regime—was used to massacre Tutsi civilians. That same month a new political party formed, the Coalition for the Defense of the Republic (CDR) even more committed to Hutu extremism than Habyarimana. It had its own militia, which was backed by the Presidential Guard and other elements of the army. France, as part of its military aid to the Rwandan government, also provided training to both militia groups—possibly without realizing it.

In June 1992 the opposition parties took the brave step of meeting with the RPF and the RPF announced that its armed struggle was over. In July a cease-fire was signed and negotiations began in Arusha, Tanzania, to set up a transitional government that would include the RPF. Habyarimana, however, blocked progress every step of the way, sometimes publicly disavowing the government negotiators at Arusha and other times organizing additional massacres.

In January 1993, an international human rights commission visited Rwanda. Its report documented abuses on all sides, but found that most of the 2,000 civilians killed were Tutsis whose murders were approved at the highest levels of the Rwandan government, including Habyarimana. As soon as the commission left the country, another 300 people were killed, and the MRND announced that it rejected the power-sharing agreement just worked out at Arusha.

The RPF responded on February 8 by breaking the cease-fire. Militarily it fared much better than before, but it declared a unilateral cease-fire on February 20, fearing possible French intervention, but probably more concerned about alienating moderate Hutus and the Hutu population generally, many of whom fled the advancing RPF troops.

France accused the RPF of unprovoked aggression—not mentioning Habyarimana's sabotaging of the Arusha talks, nor its own violation of an Arusha agreement that all foreign troops leave the country—and sent in additional soldiers and at least fifteen transport planes full of arms. On February 28, the French Minister for Cooperation called upon the opposition to make common cause with Habyarimana against the RPF, an alliance that could only be ethnically based. The opposition rejected the proposal, but Habyarimana was able to split the opposition parties, finding some elements in each party willing to join him in an extremist Hutu front.

Signs of Crisis

The signs of the approaching crisis were plain to see. The existence of death squads in Rwanda had been exposed in October 1992. The arming of the militias was regularly denounced by human rights groups. A top ideologue of the MRND was known to have given a speech in November 1992 calling for genocide. In August 1993 a UN investigator warned of the threat of ethnic killings in Rwanda. That same month, an agreement was signed at Arusha spelling out the terms of transition, but the extremists blocked its implementation. In September, members of Habyarimana's inner circle set up a new radio station, RTLM—a particularly potent medium in a country 60 percent illiterate—and used it to denounce the peace agreement and whip up ethnic hatred. In October 1993 the Hutu president of Burundi, freely elected a few months earlier, was killed in an attempted coup by extremist Tutsi army officers. Unlike 1972, the international community didn't ignore the crisis, with Washington and others suspending aid, and the coup was defeated. But Hutu extremists encouraged massacres of Tutsi peasants in the countryside and the army responded by slaughtering Hutus. All told perhaps 50,000 were killed—somewhat more Tutsis than Hutus—and 300,000 Hutus fled across the border into Rwanda, adding to the latter's ethnic tensions.

The signatories to the August Arusha agreement asked the UN to provide a neutral military force to monitor compliance. The RPF was especially eager to have the UN replace the unabashedly pro-Habyarimana French troops. In October 1993, the Security Council established the United Nations Assistance Mission in Rwanda, UNAMIR. Under strong U.S. pressure to minimize UNAMIR's size and to "seek economies," the Council deployed 2,500 Blue Helmets to Kigali. Meanwhile the French announced their withdrawal but secretly kept behind some forty to seventy soldiers.

Habyarimana continued to stall on any actual transfer of power. He was aided in this regard, perhaps inadvertently, by the U.S. ambassador and the Secretary General's special representative. Both dismissed evidence presented by the RPF of the planning going on for genocide, and both endorsed the demand by the ultra-extremist CDR for a seat in the new National Assembly. Since the CDR was openly calling for the extermination of Tutsis and denouncing the Arusha accords, urging its inclusion could only undermine the peace process and infuriated both the RPF and the democratic Hutu opposition.

Over the next few months, UNAMIR reported and protested the continued arming and training of militias, the secret importation of weapons by the government, and incendiary broadcasts on RTLM. The Belgian foreign minister described the situation as "five minutes to midnight" and warned that under its mandate UNAMIR (which included Belgian troops) could not stop the distribution of arms to civilians. No change was made in UNAMIR's mandate.

Genocide

As assassinations and mob violence spread through Kigali, intense international pressure was brought to bear on Habyarimana to accept the transitional arrangements. On April 6, 1994, Habyarimana was returning to Kigali in his presidential plane (a gift from Mitterrand), when the aircraft was shot down killing all on board. No conclusive proof is yet available as to who fired the missile, but it is almost certain that the perpetrators were Hutu extremists from Habyarimana's own inner circle. Within an hour of the plane's downing the Presidential Guard set up roadblocks throughout Kigali and proceeded to liquidate moderate Hutus whose names were on prepared lists. Among their early victims were the Hutu prime minister and ten Belgian peacekeepers. Then the militias went after every Tutsi they could find. At this point the RPF announced that it was breaking the cease-fire in order to put an end to the killings. Some later claimed that the massacres were a response to the renewed civil war, but this reverses cause and effect.

The militias were under central control at all times, and almost the entire civil service participated in the slaughter, which is what made it so efficient. This was not a case of a "failed state," then, where chaos broke out as state structures collapsed. On the contrary, it was the authoritarian state structure that carried out the killings.

With the president and the prime minister dead, the extremists announced the formation of an "interim government" consisting entirely of those committed to genocide. They hoped to convince the world that what was going on was just random interethnic violence, rather than premeditated genocide. In this they were aided by many in the West who disseminated misinformation, even though there was compelling early evidence regarding the actual nature of the killings. Ignorant journalists referred to Hutus and Tutsis "slaughter[ing] each other" and asserted that the "Hutu government does not appear to have any real control over the militiamen." Worse yet, UN Secretary General Boutros Boutros-Ghali characterized the situation more than three weeks into the genocide as one of "Hutus killing Tutsis and Tutsis killing Hutus." The next day, President Bill Clinton called on the Rwandan army and the RPF to agree to an immediate cease-fire and declared that it was "time for the leaders of Rwanda to recognize their common bond of humanity and to reject the senseless and criminal violence that continues to plague their country"—a particularly innocuous, and misleading, formulation.

One reason that events in Rwanda were characterized as interethnic killing was because this view fit nicely with Western stereotypes of savage Africans. (This was, in former New York City mayor Ed Koch's words, "tribal warfare involving those without the veneer of Western civilization.") But another reason was that U.S. officials shared with the interim government an interest in denying that genocide was taking place. As long as what was going on in Rwanda was just some mutual and chaotic killing, there was not much that Washington could be expected to do. Thus, two months after the genocide began, the Clinton administration was still instructing its officials to refrain from using the term "genocide." Not until June 15 did Clinton agree to use the term, but only because a virtually unanimous Senate Foreign Relations Committee was about to send him a letter demanding that he do so.

The real priority for the international community was evacuating its nationals from Rwanda. French paratroopers landed on April 9 and Belgians the next day. Belgium asked the UN to modify UNAMIR's mandate to allow international soldiers to stop the slaughter, but Paris rejected the idea. As part of its operation, France evacuated Habyarimana's family and—pretending they were orphanage employees—some MRND leaders. Belgian and French troops withdrew, leaving behind African partners of mixed-race couples and the French embassy's Tutsi personnel. In Washington, Senator Robert Dole declared: "I don't think we have any national interest here. I hope we don't get involved there." The "Americans are out. As far as I'm concerned in Rwanda, that ought to be the end of it."

Unable to change UNAMIR's mandate, and facing public revulsion at the killing of ten of their peacekeepers, Belgium urged the Security Council to withdraw the Blue Helmets. Washington strongly urged the total withdrawal of UNAMIR, but, finding much resistance from the Council's non-permanent members, relented and agreed to reduce the force to a token presence of 270 troops. It's hard to know what an empowered UNAMIR might have accomplished, but surely the reduction in the international presence sent a powerful message to the killers that they could murder with impunity.

U.S. officials claimed that it was the UN, not the United States, that should have done more to muster a force to prevent Rwanda's violence. But the UN cannot act independently of its most powerful members. Even when Washington does not use its veto, its economic and military strength ensure that it will be, in Phyllis Bennis's words, "calling the shots" at the UN.

The Clinton administration had earlier determined that Washington would sharply limit its support for peacekeeping operations. Clinton told the UN in September 1993 that the organization had to learn "when to say no," and to ask "hard questions" before dispatching any further peacekeeping forces. In March 1994, this new policy was formalized in Presidential Decision Directive 25. The specific tough questions that had to be answered included, in essence, being able to predict how the operations would develop, which effectively barred virtually all peacekeeping.

Some have argued that Clinton was here responding to public opinion. . . . However, in April 1995 four out of five Americans believed the UN had a responsibility to intervene in conflicts marked by genocide. Despite the obfuscation by U.S. officials as to what was going on in Rwanda, a poll taken in June and July 1994, during the genocide, found that 61 percent would have favored U.S. participation in a "large" UN force to "occupy" Rwanda and "forcibly stop the killing." . . .

Two weeks after the Council ordered the reduction in UNAMIR, the Secretary General—responding to public outrage and the insistence of some small countries—put Rwanda back on the agenda. The Council agreed to authorize a new force, UNAMIR II, 5,500 strong, for dispatch to Rwanda under an expanded mandate. However, as Human Rights Watch explained, "last minute hesitations" by Washington "resulted in orders to deploy in the first instance only a small force of several hundred troops and about 150 unarmed observers." The deployment of the rest of the force was to depend upon "progress towards a new cease-fire between the RPF and the government, the availability of resources, and further review and action" by the Council.

Some commentators have complained that no African country sent new or additional troops to Rwanda once the killing began. But these are poor countries, lacking proper equipment and the means of transporting their troops to Rwanda. On May 25, Ethiopia offered 800 troops, fully equipped and trained, but needing transportation. None was found until mid-August. Nigeria, Senegal, and Zimbabwe offered troops as well, but needed equipment. Ghana was prepared to dispatch troops as soon as they could be equipped with armored personnel carriers. Washington offered to provide these, but not for free, and the price tag would include the cost of getting them to Africa. "As the death toll mounted in Rwanda," reported the *New York Times,* the U.S. and the UN "negotiated for weeks." Not until mid-June did Washington agree to speed up the delivery. National Security Adviser Anthony Lake later boasted that "We have done what we said" and the Ghanian battalion was "about half deployed now." Unfortunately, these comments were made when the genocide was already over.

Pursuing a Cease-Fire

As African Rights [a human rights organization] argues in its powerful report, *Rwanda: Death, Despair and Defiance* (2nd edition), if UNAMIR II were used in pursuit of the same goals as were sought by U.S. and UN diplomatic efforts, the results would likely have been counterproductive as diplomatic efforts were thoroughly misguided.

In situations like Rwanda, where the bulk of the deaths are due not to military conflict, but to genocide being carried out behind the lines of one of the combatants, then a cease-fire would permit the killing to continue unimpeded. If the international community wasn't going to stop the genocide, then it had an obligation to let the RPF—the one force that could stop it—do so. Nevertheless, the thrust of international diplomacy was precisely to try to promote a cease-fire between those committing genocide and those committed to stopping it.

The RPF stated that it was willing to accept a cease-fire only if the massacres stopped. It even went along with a 96-hour cease-fire to test the international insistence that that was the way to end the genocide. The killing continued.

Significantly, one of the strongest cease-fire advocates was the genocidal regime. It wanted UNAMIR to be reinforced so that it could impose a cease-fire. This, more than anything else, should have given pause to those who called for a cease-fire. Nevertheless, on May 7 Clinton called on the Rwandan army and the RPF to agree to an immediate cease-fire, adding that it was "time for the leaders in Rwanda to reject the criminal violence that continues to plague their country," but his statement attributed neither blame for the "criminal violence" nor made its end the precondition for the cease-fire.

By the end of May, the Secretary General finally understood what was at issue: "It would be senseless to attempt to establish a cease-fire and to allow deliberate killings of civilians in the Rwandan government forces zone to continue." Therefore, "a halt to the killings of civilians must be concomitant with a cease-fire." A U.S. government statement issued the same day, however, continued the muddled policy.

A UN representative stated on April 29, 1994, that "we must not be seen to be taking sides." But as African Rights pointed out, diplomatic neutrality "was not appropriate for Rwanda." Neutrality makes sense when there is right on both sides, not when one side is committing genocide. In mid-May, the Security Council imposed an arms embargo on all parties to the conflict in Rwanda. This was inappropriate. Instead, the embargo should have been imposed on the interim government alone. This does not mean that the RPF was above criticism, only that it was the sole force capable of promptly stopping the genocide. The international community should have tried to facilitate its victory, not stall it.

Actions Not Tried

African Rights argues that in its "obsession with the despatch of troops, the international community, and specifically the United States and UN, were overlooking other courses of action" that "could have been far more effective." Here are some things that could have been tried, but were not.

First, given the dependence of Rwanda on outside aid, the international community could have made clear to the killers that no assistance would be forthcoming to a regime based on genocide. Washington resisted making such a declaration.

Second, the international community could have announced that no diplomatic recognition would be extended to a genocidal regime. Washington never made such a statement, but continued its diplomatic relations with the interim government until the RPF took Kigali. Only then did Clinton self-righteously declare that the United States "cannot allow representatives of a regime that supports genocidal massacre to remain on our soil." Even worse was the behavior of France and Egypt, which officially received and lent respectability to representatives of the interim government.

Third, the interim government could have been isolated by expelling its representative from the UN Security Council, where it ironically was permitted to retain its seat throughout the genocide. Moreover, it was allowed to participate in debate and votes on Rwanda, while the RPF was denied the opportunity to present its views.

Fourth, the leaders of the genocide were known. The international community could have identified them by name, warning them that they would be held personally accountable at war crimes trials. Washington did sometimes name the culprits and call upon them to stop the killings, but the statements did not condemn the named individuals, nor threaten them with consequences.

Fifth, France had special leverage with the interim government, being the regime's main foreign supporter. The only time Paris used its clout, it was able to stop militia members from killing people at a hotel in Kigali. As African Rights observed, this raises the prospect that "more vigorous French action could have stopped the genocide."

But if Paris was in a good position to stop the genocide, so, too, was Washington, by pressuring France. Had Clinton made a special appeal to Mitterrand to get the killers to stop, perhaps even threatening not to participate in the upcoming commemorations of the joint victory over fascism as long as France was allowing the new genocide to take place, this might have forced Paris to act. . . .

None of these alternative strategies for dealing with the genocide was pursued. Instead, embarrassed by the interminable delays in deploying UNAMIR II, the Security Council accepted an offer of a "humanitarian" military intervention from an unlikely source: France. On June 21, 1994, Paris offered to send troops to save lives until UNAMIR could arrive, but insisted that the intervention be under French command and that they not be part of UNAMIR. . . . Washington and the Secretary General endorsed the idea, but there was considerable skepticism, both inside and outside the Council.

The RPF was the most vociferous opponent of the French intervention, and this opposition led Brazil to abstain on the vote in the Security Council. New Zealand, which also abstained, sharply refuted the claim that there was no alternative to French intervention: If France were to "redirect" the resources of its intervention to transporting and equipping UNAMIR, the latter's delays would "disappear overnight."

Hesitancy by some Council members did get the enabling resolution revised to stress that the operation would be "impartial and neutral" and would "not constitute an inter-position force between the parties." Even then it only received ten affirmative votes, one more than the minimum necessary. Of the ten, one came from France, and another from the interim government of Rwanda. The latter's representative called the French initiative "timely and commendable" and urged a cease-fire.

Operation Turquoise

There were a number of motives for the French intervention, called "Operation Turquoise." This was an election year in France and politicians were competing for the high moral ground; additionally, France was receiving bad press from its complicity in the genocide, and the intervention might salvage its reputation. But there were more sinister motives as well. Jacques Baumel, vice president of the defense committee in the French National Assembly, declared that the RPF is "threatening the privileged position of France." To many French officials, the fact that the RPF had come from Uganda, where English was spoken, made it part of an "Anglo-Saxon conspiracy." Operation Turquoise, Baumel went on, has shown that France has the means to undertake "a rapid and effective intervention. Friendly countries on the black continent, and with whom we have sometimes signed treaties of military assistance can be reassured: we have just proved that we are still capable of acting in Africa. Fast and well." French troops gave Paris the ability to control events, perhaps even save the interim government.

The French government—at Prunier's suggestion—met in Paris with the RPF for the first time in the entire conflict to try to allay the latter's fears. The RPF modified its position, saying it would not oppose a purely humanitarian mission, but remained deeply suspicious. French troops were welcomed by the interim government and its army, militias, and radio; interahamwe units produced a sign proclaiming "Welcome French Hutus." Rwanda's southwestern corner, where the French forces arrived, was still under the control of the interim government. As the troops spread out into the country, their intentions remained unclear. One official declared that the RPF could not be allowed to achieve a military victory; an army captain spoke of drawing "a line in the sand"; the French defense minister declined to say how far the troops would advance or whether they would move into RPF areas; and a military spokesperson would not confirm whether French soldiers would fight the rebels in the event of a confrontation.

As it turned out, France declared the establishment of a "safe humanitarian zone" in the southwest (without waiting for UN authorization), but pulled its troops back from the northwest and the key city of Butare. The RPF agreed to halt its advance toward the zone, provided that the French disarmed all militias and military personnel there. It is possible that France's hesitations regarding the aims of Operation Turquoise were resolved by the feelings of its own troops. "This is not what we were led to believe," a noncommissioned officer said upon finding Tutsi corpses. "We were told the Tutsis were killing Hutu, and now this."

African Rights estimates that Operation Turquoise might have saved 12,000–15,000 Tutsis; Prunier reckons the number at 13,000–14,000 at most. Such numbers, of course, are nothing to sneeze at, no matter how small they seem compared to the 800,000 killed. As noted, however, France could have used its resources to equip and transport UNAMIR contingents, to save the same lives.

France allowed the organizers of the genocide to enter its safe zone and escape into Zaire without being arrested by French troops. By the time the French left, not one killer was in custody. Survivors claim they had identified major war criminals to the French forces to no avail, even though some of these criminals had been threatening people after the French arrival. Ethiopian forces who took over from the French found that some leading killers had been allowed to escape from custody and saw French vehicles being used to transport Rwandan army personnel to safety in Zaire. A BBC reporter met the former Rwandan chief of staff traveling in a French military jeep inside Zaire in late July 1994.

The organizers of the genocide wanted to escape into neighboring Zaire, but they wanted to bring with them as many of Rwanda's Hutus as possible, no matter how much suffering such a large scale population displacement might entail. A mass exodus would deny the RPF a functioning society, provide a vast sea of refugees within which the killers could hide, and allow the killers the opportunity to rebuild a military force to overthrow the victorious RPF-led regime.

To promote this mass exodus, some people were driven out by force and some followed the orders of their local officials, as they had been doing for years. But, as a UN study later concluded, the displacement of the population might have been contained had it not been for "deliberately inflammatory broadcasts from radio stations controlled by the 'interim Government'." As the RPF advanced, RTLM relocated to the French safe zone and broadcast incendiary propaganda until mid-July with no French effort to find and destroy the transmitter. (From the beginning of the genocide, human rights groups had unsuccessfully called on the UN to destroy the RTLM transmitter.) . . .

The Exodus

The architects of the genocide were successful in panicking some two million Hutus to flee Rwanda, creating a major humanitarian crisis, for there was inadequate food, water, or sanitary facilities to sustain such a massive influx of people. Cholera broke out in the refugee camps and the international community responded with a gigantic relief effort, bringing the death rate in the refugee camps to close to normal.

TV cameras transmitted the horror of the cholera epidemic on the Zairian border into the world's living rooms; the genocide in Rwanda, however, had been untelevised and thus had much less of an impact.

This led to an inaccurate public understanding of the situation, abetted by those interested in promoting confusion.

When Mitterrand was asked about the genocide, he replied: "The genocide or the genocides?" This was the double genocide gambit, the claim that there had been two genocides, one victimizing Tutsis and the other Hutus. The numbers, however, were vastly disproportionate: 800,000 Tutsis massacred and 50,000 Hutu cholera deaths. But more significant is the fact that the former were intentional deaths, the latter were not. If anyone is to be held responsible for the cholera deaths it is the interim government officials who engineered the exodus, not the Tutsi-led RPF. As Alain Destexhe, the former head of the relief agency Doctors Without Borders, wrote in his critique of the Rwanda crisis, *Rwanda and Genocide in the Twentieth Century* (New York University Press), during the slaughter of the Tutsis the word "genocide" rarely appeared in media headlines; but 'genocide' and 'Holocaust' were frequently and quite inaccurately applied, even by the most widely respected journalists, in reference to the subsequent cholera epidemic." Clinton said Rwanda could be "the world's worst humanitarian crisis in a generation," but he referred to the refugee situation, not the genocide.

The refugee camps were under the control of the very people who organized the (one and only) genocide. They acquired added leverage over the camp population through control of relief supplies. Thus, humanitarian aid had the perverse consequence of strengthening the authority of those who had been responsible for the genocide. The aid had two other negative consequences: making the living conditions in the refugee camps better than in surrounding Zaire or back home in Rwanda, thus discouraging refugees from returning home; and providing the killers with relief supplies that could be diverted and resold in order to help finance their rearming.

Doctors Without Borders closed down its program in the refugee camps so as not to be used by the killers, but for most charitable organizations the refugees in Zaire provided them with their biggest fundraising opportunity in years, and they weren't about to give it up so easily. Many of these organizations, being totally ignorant of the situation, did no screening when hiring local personnel, so numerous people implicated in the killings were on their payrolls. These individuals helped spread the extremists' message that those returning to Rwanda would be killed by the Tutsis.

Challenges Facing Rwanda's New Government

In the meantime, the victorious RPF had set up a government of national reconciliation in Rwanda. The prime minister was the Hutu chosen to be transitional prime minister as part of the 1993 Arusha accords, the president was one of the RPF's Hutu members, and most of the cabinet were Hutus. The vice-president and defense minister was Paul Kagame, the leader of the RPF's military arm, the Rwandan Patriotic Army (RPA). Despite this formal structure, however, the RPA, with the only arms, vehicles, and communications equipment in the country, was the dominant component of the new government.

The new government was faced with staggering conditions. Eight hundred thousand were dead. Among the living were untold numbers suffering from serious wounds and profound trauma. Children had been orphaned, spouses widowed, women raped. In some areas just about every Tutsi house had been demolished. Many who had participated in the killings were still around. There was no police force. There was no court system. Yet trials of the perpetrators of the massacres were essential, both to break the culture of impunity which had flourished for so long in Rwanda, and to answer the victims' cry for justice, without which there was the grave danger of private retribution. The RPA needed to remain mobilized, given the continuing threat on the borders from the troops of the former regime, yet the new government lacked even the funds to pay its soldiers.

If ever there were a government in need of massive international assistance, both financial and technical, this was it. Yet, as a top official at the U.S. Agency for International Development remarked in September 1994, he had never witnessed a situation in which the international community had essentially marginalized a government to the extent it had in Rwanda. While millions of dollars poured into the refugee camps dominated by the killers, hardly any money went to the Rwandan government. The new prime minister was baffled: "We appreciate what is happening to help the dying in the camps. But beyond that, what? Must we get cholera to be helped?"

International donors told the Rwandan government that aid was contingent on its making conditions within the country secure for the return of the refugees. But security required precisely the aid that was being withheld. Numerous human rights reports had found no evidence of genocide or systematic atrocities on the part of the RPF. The RPF had maintained fairly good discipline and had generally restrained revenge killings on the part of its members. But as the destitution of the Rwandan government continued, the situation worsened. Unpaid soldiers began to hire themselves out to settle private vendettas. Tutsi supremacists began to gain in strength.

African Rights argues that the UN's Human Rights Field Operation viewed its mission not as helping to deal with the aftermath of the genocide by bringing the perpetrators to justice, but as single-mindedly seeking out human rights violations by the RPF. Some of the human rights monitors bitterly complained to African Rights that they were being told that their job was "nailing the RPA." They had no problem, they said, with exposing and criticizing RPA violations, but they resented the fact that this had become their exclusive task. And Rwandan survivors of the genocide resented this even more.

The Security Council set up a war crimes tribunal to deal with the Rwandan genocide, but it was much delayed and underfunded. The enabling resolution—as Lawyers Without Borders and the Rwandan government noted—was worded so as to exclude from the scope of the tribunal's consideration various crimes: among them, crimes committed before January 1, 1994 (for example, the drawing up of lists of victims in 1993); crimes committed outside of Rwanda by non-Rwandans (for example, French citizens who delivered arms to Zaire, for shipment to the interim government in Rwanda); and crimes committed by states, effectively letting France and Zaire off the hook.

The international tribunal issued its first indictments in December 1995, but the whereabouts of the eight indictees was unknown. The Security Council "urged"—but did not require—states to arrest and detain potential war criminals; few are likely to actually stand trial. . . .

America's Record in Rwanda

Rwanda has experienced, in the words of Boutros-Ghali, "what would have been a nightmare had it not actually come to pass." And other nations bear a deep responsibility for that nightmare. On July 26, 1994, after the genocide was over, U.S. Assistant Secretary of State for African Affairs George Moose told a Senate committee: "Through the UN, the United States has taken a leading role in efforts to protect the Rwandan people. We strongly supported the UN arms embargo and the expansion of UNAMIR, with a revised mandate to help protect threatened populations and relief efforts." No mention was made of the U.S. refusal to expose those who were providing arms to the killers, of the U.S.-led effort to reduce UNAMIR, of the U.S.-inspired delays in deploying UNAMIR II, of the U.S. insistence on a cease-fire, of the U.S. refusal to call genocide "genocide," to pressure Paris, or to isolate the genocidal regime. France is the foreign country bearing primary culpability for Rwanda's nightmare, but there is little in the record of the United States of which to be proud.

Surviving the Genocide in Rwanda: Personal Accounts

Philip Gourevitch

Hundreds of thousands of citizens of the small African nation of Rwanda were slaughtered between April and July 1994; most of the victims were members of the minority Tutsi ethnic group. In the following excerpt from his book *We Wish to Inform You That Tomorrow We Will Be Killed With Our Families*, Philip Gourevitch recounts the experiences of two Tutsi survivors of the genocide. The two men describe the bloody massacre of approximately two thousand Tutsis who had sought refuge in a church hospital in a hilltop village. Gourevitch is a journalist and staff writer for the *New Yorker* magazine.

If you could walk due west from the massacre memorial at Nyarubuye, straight across Rwanda from one end to the other, over the hills and through the marshes, lakes, and rivers to the province of Kibuye, then, just before you fell into the great inland sea of Lake Kivu, you would come to another hilltop village. This hill is called Mugonero, and it, too, is crowned by a big church. While Rwanda is overwhelmingly Catholic, Protestants evangelized much of Kibuye, and Mugonero is the headquarters of the Seventh-Day Adventist mission. The place resembles the brick campus of an American community college more than an African village; tidy tree-lined footpaths connect the big church with a smaller chapel, a nursing school, an infirmary, and a hospital complex that enjoyed a reputation for giving excellent medical care. It was in the hospital that Samuel Ndagijimana sought refuge during the killings, and although one of the first things he said to me was "I forget bit by bit," it quickly became clear that he hadn't forgotten as much as he might have liked.

Samuel worked as a medical orderly in the hospital. He had landed the job in 1991, when he was twenty-five. I asked him about his life in that time that Rwandans call "Before." He said, "We were simple Christians." That was all. I might have been asking about someone else, whom he had met only in passing, and who didn't interest him. It was as if his first real memory was of the early days in April of 1994 when he saw Hutu militiamen conducting public exercises outside the government offices in Mugonero. "We watched young people going out every night, and people spoke of it on the radio," Samuel said. "It was only members of Hutu Power parties who went out, and those who weren't participants were called 'enemies.'"

On April 6, a few nights after this activity began, Rwanda's long-standing Hutu dictator, President Juvénal Habyarimana, was assassinated in Kigali, and a clique of Hutu Power leaders from the military high command seized power. "The radio announced that people shouldn't move," Samuel said. "We began to see groups of people gathering that same night, and when we went to work in the morning, we saw these groups with the local leaders of Hutu Power organizing the population. You didn't know exactly what was happening, just that there was something coming."

At work, Samuel observed "a change of climate." He said that "one didn't talk to anyone anymore," and many of his co-workers spent all their time in meetings with a certain Dr. Gerard, who made no secret of his support for Hutu Power. Samuel found this shocking, because Dr. Gerard had been trained in the United States, and he was the son of the president of the Adventist church in Kibuye, so he was seen as a figure of great authority, a community leader—one who sets the example.

After a few days, when Samuel looked south across the valley from Mugonero, he saw houses burning in villages along the lakefront. He decided to stay in the church hospital until the troubles were over, and Tutsi families from Mugonero and surrounding areas soon began arriving with the same idea. This was a tradition in Rwanda. "When there were problems, people always went to the church," Samuel said. "The pastors were Christians. One trusted that nothing would happen at their place." In fact, many people at Mugonero told me that Dr. Gerard's father, the church president, Pastor Elizaphan Ntakirutimana, was personally instructing Tutsis to gather at the Adventist complex.

Wounded Tutsis converged on Mugonero from up and down the lake. They came through the bush, trying to avoid the countless militia checkpoints along the road, and they brought stories. Some told how a few miles to the north, in Gishyita, the mayor had been so frantic in his impatience to kill Tutsis that thousands had been slaughtered even as he herded them to the church, where the remainder were massacred. Others told how a few miles to the south, in Rwamatamu, more than ten thousand Tutsis had taken refuge in the town hall, and the mayor had brought in truckloads of policemen and soldiers and militia with guns and grenades to surround the place; behind them he had arranged villagers with machetes in case anyone escaped when the shooting began—and, in fact, there had been very few escapees from Rwamatamu. An Adventist pastor and his son were said to have worked closely with the mayor in organizing the slaughter at Rwamatamu. But perhaps

Samuel did not hear about that from the wounded he met, who came "having been shot at, and had grenades thrown, missing an arm, or a leg." He still imagined that Mugonero could be spared.

By April 12, the hospital was packed with as many as two thousand refugees, and the water lines were cut. Nobody could leave; militiamen and members of the Presidential Guard had cordoned off the complex. But when Dr. Gerard learned that several dozen Hutus were among the refugees, he arranged for them to be evacuated. He also locked up the pharmacy, refusing treatment to the wounded and sick—"because they were Tutsi," Samuel said. Peering out from their confines, the refugees at the hospital watched Dr. Gerard and his father, Pastor Ntakirutimana, driving around with militiamen and members of the Presidential Guard. The refugees wondered whether these men had forgotten their God.

Among the Tutsis at the Mugonero church and hospital complex were seven Adventist pastors who quickly assumed their accustomed role as leaders of the flock. When two policemen turned up at the hospital, and announced that their job was to protect the refugees, the Tutsi pastors took up a collection, and raised almost four hundred dollars for the policemen. For several days, all was calm. Then, toward evening on April 15, the policemen said they had to leave because the hospital was to be attacked the next morning. They drove away in a car with Dr. Gerard, and the seven pastors in the hospital advised their fellow refugees to expect the end. Then the pastors sat down together and wrote letters to the mayor and to their boss, Pastor Elizaphan Ntakirutimana, Dr. Gerard's father, asking them in the name of the Lord to intercede on their behalf.

"And the response came," Samuel said. "It was Dr. Gerard who announced it: 'Saturday, the sixteenth, at exactly nine o'clock in the morning, you will be attacked.'" But it was Pastor Ntakirutimana's response that crushed Samuel's spirit, and he repeated the church president's words twice over, slowly: "Your problem has already found a solution. You must die." One of Samuel's colleagues, Manase Bimenyimana, remembered Ntakirutimana's response slightly differently. He told me that the pastor's words were "You must be eliminated. God no longer wants you."

In his capacity as a hospital orderly, Manase served as the household domestic for one of the doctors, and he had remained at the doctor's house after installing his wife and children—for safety—among the refugees at the hospital. Around nine o'clock on the morning of Saturday, April 16, he was feeding the doctor's dogs. He saw Dr. Gerard drive toward the hospital with a carload of armed men. Then he heard shooting and grenades exploding. "When the dogs heard the cries of the people," he told me, "they too began to howl."

Manase managed to make his way to the hospital—foolishly, perhaps, but he felt exposed and wanted to be with his family. He found the Tutsi pastors instructing the refugees to prepare for death. "I was very disappointed," Manase said. "I expected to die, and we started looking for anything to defend ourselves with—stones, broken bricks, sticks. But they were useless. The people were weak. They had nothing to eat. The shooting started, and people were falling down and dying."

There were many attackers, Samuel recalled, and they came from all sides—"from the church, from behind, from the north and south. We heard shots and cries and they chanted the slogan 'Eliminate the Tutsis.' They began shooting at us, and we threw stones at them because we had nothing else, not even a machete. We were hungry, tired, we hadn't had water for more than a day. There were people who had their arms cut off. There were dead. They killed the people at the chapel and the school and then the hospital. I saw Dr. Gerard, and I saw his father's car pass the hospital and stop near his office. Around noon, we went into a basement. I was with some family members. Others had been killed already. The attackers began to break down the doors and to kill, shooting and throwing grenades. The two policemen who had been our protectors were now attackers. The local citizenry also helped. Those who had no guns had machetes or *masus*. In the evening, around eight or nine o'clock, they began firing tear gas. People who were still alive cried. That way the attackers knew where people were, and they could kill them directly."

On the national average, Tutsis made up a bit less than fifteen percent of Rwanda's population, but in the province of Kibuye the balance between Hutus and Tutsis was close to fifty-fifty. On April 6, 1994, about a quarter million Tutsis lived in Kibuye and a month later more than two hundred thousand of them had been killed. In many of Kibuye's villages, no Tutsis survived.

Manase told me that he was surprised when he heard that "only a million people" were killed in Rwanda. "Look at how many died just here, and how many were eaten by birds," he said. It was true that the dead of the genocide had been a great boon to Rwanda's birds, but the birds had also been helpful to the living. Just as birds of prey and carrion will form a front in the air before the advancing wall of a forest fire to feast on the parade of animals fleeing the inferno, so in Rwanda during the months of extermination the kettles of buzzards, kites, and crows that boiled over massacre sites marked a national map against the sky, flagging the "no-go" zones for people like Samuel and Manase, who took to the bush to survive.

Sometime before midnight on April 16, the killers at the Mugonero Adventist complex, unable to discover anybody left there to kill, went off to loot the homes of the dead, and Samuel in his basement, and Manase hiding with his murdered wife and children, found themselves unaccountably alive. Manase left immediately. He made his way to the nearby village of Murambi, where he joined up with a small band of survivors from other massacres who had once more taken shelter in an Adventist church. For nearly twenty-four hours, he said, they had peace. Then Dr. Gerard came with a convoy of militia. Again there was shooting, and Manase escaped. This time, he fled high up into the mountains, to a place called Bisesero, where the rock is steep and craggy, full of caves and often swaddled in cloud. Bisesero was the only place in Rwanda where thousands of Tutsi civilians mounted a defense against the Hutus who were trying to kill them. "Looking at how many people there were in Bisesero, we were convinced we could not die," Manase told me. And at first, he said, "only women and children were killed, because the men were fighting." But in time tens of thousands of men fell there, too.

Down in the corpse-crowded villages of Kibuye, live Tutsis had become extremely hard to find. But the killers never gave up. The hunt was in Bisesero, and the hunters came by truck and bus. "When they saw how strong the resistance was, they called militias from far away," Manase said. "And they did not kill simply. When we were weak, they saved bullets and killed us with bamboo spears. They cut Achilles tendons and necks, but not completely, and then they left the victims to spend a long time crying until they died. Cats and dogs were there, just eating people."

Samuel, too, had found his way to Bisesero. He had lingered in the Mugonero hospital, "full of dead," until one in the morning. Then he crept out of the basement and, carrying "one who had lost his feet," he proceeded slowly into the mountains. Samuel's account of his ordeal following the slaughter at his workplace was as telegraphic as his description of life in Mugonero before the genocide. Unlike Manase, he found little comfort at Bisesero, where the defenders' only advantage was the terrain. He had concluded that to be a Tutsi in Rwanda meant death. "After a month," he said, "I went to Zaire." To get there he had to descend through settled areas to Lake Kivu, and to cross the water at night in a pirogue—an outrageously risky journey, but Samuel didn't mention it.

Manase remained in Bisesero. During the fighting, he told me, "we got so used to running that when one wasn't running one didn't feel right." Fighting and running gave Manase spirit, a sense of belonging to a purpose greater than his own existence. Then he got shot in the thigh, and life once again became about little more than staying alive. He found a cavern, "a rock where a stream went underground, and came out below," and made it his home. "By day, I was alone," he said. "There were only dead people. The bodies fell down in the stream, and I used those bodies as a bridge to cross the water and join the other people in the evenings." In this way, Manase survived.

CHAPTER 2

EXPLAINING GENOCIDE

Contemporary Issues
Companion

DEFINING GENOCIDE

David Rieff

David Rieff is the author of *Slaughterhouse: Bosnia and the Failure of the West* and of numerous articles published in *Foreign Affairs,* the *New Yorker,* and other periodicals. In the following essay, he briefly recounts the history of the word *genocide,* which was coined in 1944 by Polish scholar Raphael Lemkin. Rieff also discusses the definition given by the Convention on the Prevention and Punishment of the Crime of Genocide, which was passed by the United Nations in 1948. The 1948 convention mandates that signatory nations are obligated to intervene to stop genocides. However, Rieff explains, varying definitions have made it difficult to distinguish a genocidal campaign of extermination from other acts of violence, such as civil war. Rieff writes that both overly broad and overly restrictive conceptions as to what constitutes genocide have contributed to this confusion, allowing nations to avoid their moral responsibility to stop such atrocities.

The Convention on the Prevention and Punishment of the Crime of Genocide, originally known as Resolution 260A (III) of the United Nations General Assembly, was passed on December 9, 1948, and came into effect as a binding piece of international law on January 12, 1951. Since 1948, it has been ratified by 120 countries. Its provisions are broad. The definition of genocide obviously includes campaigns to exterminate entire peoples, but the framers of the Convention emphasized that genocide was "the intent to destroy, in whole or in part, a national, ethnical, racial, or religious group." The "in part" is crucial, as is the language in the Convention that states that a genocide need not be accomplished through mass murder to qualify as genocide. Any of the following acts—"killing members of the group; causing serious bodily or mental harm to members of the group; deliberately inflicting on the group conditions of life calculated to bring about its physical destruction in whole or in part; imposing measures intended to prevent births within the group; forcibly transferring children of the group to another group"—are sufficient to substantiate the claim that a genocide is taking place, and to impose on the Convention's signatories an affirmative obligation to intervene to stop it.

Excerpted from David Rieff, *The Rwanda Crisis: History of a Genocide.* Reprinted from an article originally published in *The New Republic.* © David Rieff. Reprinted with the permission of The Wylie Agency, Inc.

The Convention asserts that genocide is a crime that has existed "in all periods of history." And yet clearly, like so many of the founding documents of the United Nations, its language is haunted by the memory of Nazism. The founders of the U.N., as Dag Hammarsjkold once remarked, created the organization not to bring mankind to heaven, but to save it from hell. And genocide seemed like a paradigmatic instance of the kind of evil that, unlike war itself, the "civilized world" (as the framers of the Convention unself-consciously called it) could ban, just as piracy and poison gas had been banned (and mostly stamped out) by previous international edicts. If genocide had always existed, the framers of the Convention also seemed to assert, somewhat contradictorily, that it was something new, something modern. In the linguistic sense, they were right. Until 1944, the word "genocide" did not exist. Toward the end of the Second World War, as the full realization of what had happened in the concentration camps was becoming clear, Winston Churchill had written that the world was being confronted with "a crime that has no name." He was wrong, but only barely. At roughly the same time, Raphael Lemkin, a jurist, Polish-born and Jewish, who was working as an adviser to the United States War Department, had coined the term "genocide," and used it in his book *Axis Rule in Occupied Europe.* "New conceptions," Lemkin wrote, "require new terms." For Lemkin, genocide meant the destruction of a nation or ethnic group—though not, as he would emphasize, its total extermination. In this sense, it was "an old practice in its modern development." To describe it, he invented a neologism, cobbled together from the Greek word genos (race or tribe) and the Latin suffix cide (to kill).

Lemkin's Conception of Genocide

Lemkin was aware that there were many historical examples of wars of extermination, and in a footnote he adduced examples from the destruction of Carthage to the massacre of the Albigensians. But for him a war of extermination and a genocide were not exactly synonymous. In 1944, he knew about the extermination of the Jews, even if he did not realize the full extent of what the Germans had done— Lemkin estimated that 1,700,000 Jews had been murdered—but he resisted that genocide need not be a master plan for the physical extermination of a people or a group. A genocide could take place even when it was employed partially, as a method of weakening rather than murdering all the members of a people. This kind of genocide, Lemkin thought, was being widely practiced by the German occupiers. In the east, particularly in Poland and Western Russia, it was a way of ensuring that "the German people would be stronger than the subjugated peoples after the war even if the German army is defeated."

Lemkin already understood that the Germans had been waging war "not merely against states and their armies but against peoples." Until

Hitler came to power, the evolution of the history of war had been in the opposite direction, largely limited to activities against armies and states. In World War I, the ratio of military to civilian dead was 90:10. In World War II, sixty-seven civilians died for every ten soldiers. And the ratio worldwide is now the exact opposite of what it was at the beginning of the 1914–1918 war: ninety civilians for every ten soldiers. The "long period of evolution in civilized society," in which Lemkin discerned a steady aversion to wars of extermination, had been reversed by the Germans. Genocide was thus not only a crime against humanity, it was also a threat to future generations, unless the world committed itself to its prevention. Lemkin was not a naive One-Worlder. "Many hope that there will be no more wars," he wrote, "but we dare not rely on mere hopes for protection against genocidal practices by ruthless conquerors." And far from believing, as so many people in Europe and America did when the genocide of the Bosnian Muslims began in 1992, that after Hitler there would be no more genocides in Europe, Lemkin saw genocide not only as a problem of the Second World War, but, even more crucially, as a problem of the postwar peace. Genocide, he wrote, "is an especially important problem for Europe, where differentiation in nationhood is so marked that despite the principle of political and territorial self-determination, certain national groups may be obliged to live as minorities within the boundaries of other states. If these groups should not be adequately protected, such lack of protection would result in international disturbances, especially in the form of disorganized emigration of the persecuted, who would look for refuge elsewhere."

After the war, it was Lemkin who almost single-handedly succeeded in bringing about the passage of the Genocide Convention. Today, in the wake of the Bosnian slaughter, anyone wanting to think seriously about the problem of genocide needs to return to Lemkin, to his expansive definition of genocide and his clearheaded realization that it represented not only a moral threat but also a strategic threat. For, fifty years later, Lemkin's worst fears have been realized. By his definition, we seem to have entered what might be called an age of genocide—a period in which the goal of wars will be first and foremost the expulsion or the murder of members of a racial, religious, or ethnic group, and their replacement by members of the murdering or expelling group, rather than the military victory of one state over another.

Lemkin allowed himself to hope. He put his faith in the nascent United Nations and in the power of international law. Even before the Second World War, he had been campaigning for a unified international criminal law in which crimes of "barbarity," offenses against individuals because of their membership in a national, religious, or racial group, and "vandalism," the destruction of works of art embodying "the genius" of the other group, would be added to the penal code. And his hope that a genuine international community could be forged out of the experience of World War II was shared by many in 1944 and 1945. If today the United Nations seems like little more than a waste of hope, this should not be held against Lemkin. In any case, Lemkin's original definition of genocide, as opposed to the way the Genocide Convention has subsequently been understood, and the way Lemkin's intellectual inheritors and popularizers have interpreted his work, is notable for its modesty. Lemkin never claimed that only a crime on the order of the Nazi Holocaust was a genocide. He made no requirement that the genocide be total; nor was he concerned with establishing a quantitative threshold, a number of victims below which the word "genocide" could not be employed. Lemkin emphasized over and over again that the offense against a group could be total or partial. The fate of the Bosnian Muslims would certainly have qualified as genocide under this definition. When Lemkin writes that "even before the war Hitler envisaged genocide as a means of changing the biological interrelations in Europe in Germany," he could as well have been writing about the designs of Yugoslavian president Slobodan Milosevic and Bosnian Serb leader Radovan Karadzic. They, too, did not insist on killing every Bosnian Muslim. To the contrary, the Bosnian Serb campaign of ethnic cleansing and mass murder was conducted most brutally in those areas where there was either a Muslim majority or where the Serb-Muslim population ratio was at near parity. Where Serbs were in the overwhelming majority, Muslims were usually left alone.

For Lemkin, mass killing was only part of what made a whole range of barbaric acts committed by a belligerent in war a *genocide*. Genocide, he wrote, was "a composite of different acts of persecution or destruction." There were two phases: "one, destruction of the national pattern of the oppressed group; the other, the imposition of the national pattern of the oppressor." Again, a premonition of Bosnia. The Serb campaign of rape against Bosnian Muslim women was an element in such a campaign of destruction; and so, more broadly, was ethnic cleansing. The Serb effort to eradicate the traces of Islam from all the territories their forces controlled, and to replace the mosques with Orthodox churches, as well as the renaming of towns, was typical of Lemkin's second phase.

An Abused Term

In the postwar period, Lemkin's definition of genocide was subtly altered. This occurred in part during the negotiations that culminated in the passage of the Genocide Convention. But the change has also been a cultural one. If 6 million deaths was too exacting a criterion for the ascription of genocide, was any organized campaign of affront against a national, racial, or religious group a genocide? Can there be genocide without violence? Some Americans think so, and since the

1960s the term has been used with increasing sloppiness and tendentiousness, and has been made into a metaphor. Talk of "cultural" and "spiritual" genocide has become a part of the rhetorical landscape, particularly in our carnival of identity politics. As Alain Destexhe, one of the founders of Medecins Sans Frontieres (MSF) (Doctors Without Borders), observes in his remarkable book, *Rwanda and Genocide in the Twentieth Century,* genocide has "progressively lost its initial meaning and is becoming dangerously commonplace." Destexhe is Lemkin's faithful and eloquent disciple. His book is a polemic that calls unabashedly for a return to the most austere and limited definition of genocide. "In order to shock people into paying attention to contemporary situations that reflect varying degrees of violence or injustice by making comparisons with murder on the greatest scale known in this century, [genocide] has been used in ways synonymous with massacre, oppression, and repression, overlooking the fact that the image it conjures up was an attempt to annihilate the whole Jewish race." His aim, Destexhe insists, "is to restore the specific meaning to a term which has been so much abused that it has become the victim of its own success." . . .

Destexhe worries about the debasement of language and the distortions of a media-saturated culture. And so he insists on strict constructions. In a world in which every crime can be called a genocide—the "hunger holocaust" is one example of verbal inflation that particularly infuriates him—how can there be a serious morality or a serious rationality? Destexhe proposes that the term "genocide" be limited to situations where all counts enumerated in the Genocide Convention apply, and to no others. "Genocide," he writes, "must be reinstated as the most infamous of crimes, the memory of victims preserved and those responsible identified and brought to justice by the international community." This anger is tonic and necessary, and it comes from a different intellectual and moral universe than that which informs most writing on genocide. The sentimentality and the lack of grounding in real experience, the weakness for thinking metaphorically about the most concrete of human tragedies, the Jimmy Carter–like need to understand everyone's point of view—all tendencies that are exemplified by the work on genocide of Robert Jay Lifton and others—are wholly absent from Destexhe's discussion. His moralism is based on the need to make distinctions between tragedies. When Auschwitz equals Hiroshima, and Hiroshima equals Dresden, and the crimes of the Waffen SS equal the crimes of the Americans in Vietnam, Destexhe insists, "the real meaning of genocide will continue to be trivialized, and this most antihuman of all crimes will continue to be regarded as one more reason to justify fatalism."

Destexhe's book is the cry of a man in despair, an extraordinary meditation on the nature of human solidarity and individual responsibility in this era of mass murder. . . . . It is not clear, however, that Destexhe's attempt in his book to define genocide in a manner so restrictive that only three twentieth-century events can be called genocides—the massacre of the Armenians by the Turks in 1915; the Jewish Holocaust between 1939 and 1945; and the extermination of the Rwandan Tutsis in 1994—is intellectually or morally sustainable. Indeed, it could be argued that, if one returns to Lemkin's original definition, Destexhe's claim that there have only been three "genuine" genocides is far too restrictive. It may even be that his definition is, in its own way, almost as much of a misuse of the term as are those wanton uses—"cultural genocide," "hunger holocaust"—that he rightly deplores.

Destexhe does not so much want to return to Lemkin as to the definition of genocide as it was understood in the late 1940s. At that time genocide was commonly understood as a peculiarly modern and Western contribution to the history of barbarism. Of course, the preamble of the Genocide Convention acknowledges that "at all periods of history genocide has inflicted great losses on humanity." But what its framers clearly have in mind is the Holocaust. In the late 1940s, this made sense. And yet, in retrospect, it is not clear that the term "genocide"—as opposed to "Shoah" or "Holocaust," words specific to what happened in Europe between 1941 and 1945 that need never lose their appositeness or their force—could long have retained its moral and conceptual coherence as Hitler's war receded from living memory.

Hitler's Unique Crime

For even as a genocide, Hitler's crime was unique. To eradicate European Jewry, Hitler sacrificed everything else, including the resupply of his forces on the Russian front. There are times in Destexhe's book where he seems on the verge of insisting that there have only been two genocides, of the Jews and of the Tutsis. Were he to have made that argument, his book would have an intellectual consistency that it does not otherwise possess. He wants to insist that genocide is "the most infamous of crimes," but he excludes from his definition not only the Serb campaign against the Bosnian Muslims, but also Stalin's terror famine, Pol Pot's campaign of mass murder and, on a numerically though in no sense culturally smaller scale, the extermination of various Amazonian tribes. Leave aside for the moment the quantitative question of whether a crime that leaves more people dead than any of the genocides by which Destexhe is haunted can really be considered a lesser evil. Destexhe counts the Armenian tragedy as a genocide. But does it fit his own horrific paradigm? For what the Turks did was not nearly as all-encompassing as what the Nazis did. For a start, the Turkish authorities did not try to kill every Armenian everywhere that Ottoman power held sway. Quite the contrary. The mass extinction of the Armenians of northeastern Anatolia was carefully planned and carried out, and the Turkish authorities wished to eliminate, through murder and mass expulsion (what the Serbs have taught us to call "ethnic cleansing") the Armenian presence in most of the country—and yet the substantial Armenian populations of Smyrna and Constantinople were by and large left alone, and those few Armenians from the northeast who managed to reach the Turkish Aegean were neither hunted nor attacked.

The fact that not all Armenians were killed has been used by Turkish apologists to buttress their obscene denials that a genocide took place. What is most interesting about the Turkish denials is that the Nazi example is often used to support a claim of innocence. Thus the Holocaust may have come not only to define the issue, but also to confuse it. If one principal characteristic of genocide is extermination carried out with absolute single-mindedness, even to the detriment of the genocidal state's other policies and ambitions, and if the other principal characteristic is numerical, then genocide will never really be understood except insofar as it approaches or falls away from the Holocaust. And in this way the Holocaust may be used to exonerate many crimes and many criminals. . . .

The Power of Words

It is not clear whether Destexhe is trapped by his understanding of Lemkin's original definition, or is simply at his wit's end in finding a way to combat the indifference that a latitudinarian definition of genocide has engendered in the West. But his passion leads him to misstatements of fact. Destexhe's implicit (and correct) insistence on the radical, unique evil of Hitler's war against the Jews is contradicted by his own characterization of it as "murder on the greatest scale known in this century." If we are discussing scale, then it is important to remember that on purely numerical grounds the 1932–33 famine that Soviet Union leader Joseph Stalin visited on the Ukraine was responsible for more deaths than the death camps and the Einsatzgruppen Nazi mobile killing squads. Such a comparison may seem a little obscene, but this is really the fault of those, such as Destexhe and the other "strict constructionists" of genocide, who have set up a quantitative standard. Other, unquantitative conceptions of genocide are possible. And they are not so strict that they are useless. It is unlikely that most of the crimes in which genocidal killing and genocidally motivated campaigns of rape, vandalism, and expulsion take place will be as total as what took place in Nazi-occupied Europe or in Rwanda. Destexhe, like Lemkin, argues that a strict definition of genocide will make people less complacent, more inclined to help bring the perpetrators of the few real genocides to justice. I do not think that he is right. It seems more probable that such an infrequently instantiated notion of ultimacy will make people more complacent, as they dismiss the overwhelming number of crimes that do not correspond to the exacting definition. If I am right, and we are entering a time in which genocide will become more and more commonplace, there will be enough fatalism around without buttressing it with the moral excuse that Cambodia, or East Bengal, or Bosnia, or South Sudan, is not Auschwitz or Nyarubyue Mission. In the matter of genocide, strictness of definition can have the same unfortunate effect as sloppiness of definition. Our sense of genocide must be as flexible and as inventive as the human capacity for evil.

Raphael Lemkin coined the word "genocide" as a way of facilitating historical understanding. If the word helps us to come to grips with Rwanda, or Bosnia, or other crimes and tragedies that await us, if it helps us to remember, as Gerard Prunier puts it in the foreword to his book, *The Rwanda Crisis*, that "what we have witnessed in Rwanda is a historical product, not a biological fatality or a 'spontaneous' bestial outburst," then let us continue to rely upon it. But the word was always a moral and intellectual shorthand, a necessary but futile attempt to master evil by describing it. If the word itself has become a kind of mystification, a way of forcing the bitterest of human experiences into hierarchies of suffering that no longer make much moral or practical sense, then there is no reason to cling to it. Its referent, anyway, will be with us. The victims will still be there, as will the need for human solidarity, without whose rebirth our world will soon become morally uninhabitable.

HOW PEOPLE ARE PERSUADED TO COMMIT GENOCIDE

Herbert Hirsch

Mass murders such as the Holocaust cannot take place without the consensus and efforts of many people, writes Herbert Hirsch in the following excerpt from his book *Genocide and the Politics of Memory: Studying Death to Preserve Life*. Planners of genocide must create certain conditions that enable people to commit atrocities that they ordinarily would not consider and to avoid feeling guilt, pain, or empathy when they destroy the lives of others. Hirsch identifies and describes three broad types of conditions—cultural, psychological, and political—through which genocide is made possible. For example, he explains, populations targeted for elimination are dehumanized through propaganda in order to provide a rationale for their extermination.

"So you didn't feel they were human beings?"
"Cargo . . . they were cargo."
"There were so many children, did they ever make you think of your children, of how you would feel in the position of those parents?"
"No . . . I can't say I ever thought this way. . . . You see . . . I rarely saw them as individuals. It was always as a huge mass."
—Franz Stangl, commandant of Sobibor and Treblinka extermination camps, interviewed by Gitta Sereny, *Into That Darkness* (1974)

As memory is transmitted from generation to generation in the ongoing process of renewing the species, the myths, legends, and other assorted likes and dislikes that persist in a culture are also transmitted. . . . If memory is to serve as a warning and to act as the foundation on which to build a more humane world, it is important to understand how people become killers. The bluntest possible confrontation with the most depressing possibilities is called for so as not to disguise the realities. We must, therefore, begin with the realization that mass murder does not occur in a vacuum and is not committed by "other" people. For people to die, other people have to pull

the triggers, release the gas, and drop the bombs. How they are convinced to undertake such actions knowing full well what the end
result will be is a question of enduring significance. The search for
answers might very well begin with a consideration of Raul Hilberg's
classic work, *The Destruction of the European Jews.*

Hilberg notes that in order for mass murder to occur, mechanisms
must be developed to short-circuit traditional concepts of individual
morality. Psychologically, people must not be allowed to feel guilt or
pain, or empathy, when they destroy others. . . .

Mechanisms are developed to justify and rationalize the destruction
of the targeted group. In short, the planners of the proposed massacres
must motivate participation in order to bring about the desired
result—extermination. To accomplish this, certain conditions must be
created. These conditions, as we shall see, allow the perpetrators to
successfully carry out their planned actions while at the same time
providing a means to dissipate guilt and explain why such horrible
acts were necessary. . . .

[There are] three conditions under which the state will be able to
motivate participation in mass murder. Lacking more descriptive terminology, I call them cultural, psychological, and political conditions.

Cultural Conditions

Cultural conditions are usually tied to the myths and ideologies
stressed in a culture or a nation-state, which are used to rationalize
or justify the destructive activity of the state. . . . Every society
claims a genealogy, an explanation grounded in mythology of the
origin of its people or of the state. Generally, these myths hold that
the members of the group or the state descend from divine sources
or are protected by divine intervention. This type of thinking differ-
entiates the group or the state from all other groups or states and
thus serves as a reason for dehumanizing those perceived as "the
enemy," against whom the state wishes to pursue aggressive action.
The fact that "enemies" are not protected by or descended from the
same bloodlines and do not have the same pedigree may serve as a
justification for genocide.

In other words, the myths and ideologies stressed in a culture or
state are expressed in the language of the major authority figures and
are transmitted, through the process of acculturation or socialization,
to the people living within the bounds of the state. As they absorb and
begin to believe these myths, they are conditioned so that when
ordered to engage in acts they might not have considered moral in
other circumstances, they are willing to obey the orders because of the
elaborate system of justification that has been constructed. These cultural conditions for mass murder are related to psychological conditions, which focus on the explicit mechanisms through which citizens
are taught to obey authority.

Psychological Conditions

The psychological conditions for participation in acts of atrocity focus directly on the possibility that, given certain circumstances, individuals might find themselves in a position in which their sense of individual morality, of right and wrong, is compromised. The basic psychological conditions necessary for mass murder involve obedience to authority; following orders takes precedence over all other considerations. Under these conditions, individuals no longer view themselves as responsible for their actions, and they define themselves as instruments for carrying out the wishes and commands of those in positions of authority. The classic example, of course, is [Nazi official and war criminal] Adolf Eichmann.

After his [1960] arrest for war crimes, Eichmann never expressed guilt or remorse for the acts he committed. His position, according to the transcripts of his interrogation, was that he had never killed any Jews: "I had nothing to do with killing the Jews. I never killed a Jew, but I never killed a non-Jew either—I've never killed anybody. And I never ordered anybody to kill a Jew, or ordered anybody to kill a non-Jew. No, never." Eichmann, however, left little doubt that if he had received such an order he would have done so. In fact, he recalled that he would have felt remorse only if he had not done what he had been ordered to do—that is, organize the transportation of millions of men, women, and children to their death "with great zeal and meticulous care," as writer Hannah Arendt states. Eichmann has become the prototype of the person whose sense of individual morality has been reoriented so that he or she feels shame or pride according to how efficiently he or she carries out orders. Efficiency in carrying out orders remains a highly desired value in contemporary society. In fact, social scientist Stanley Milgram has argued that morality takes on a different shape in the highly bureaucratized, hierarchical states that characterize our times. Morality is now defined, as it was for Eichmann, in terms of how well a person carries out the tasks assigned to him or her—no matter what they may entail.

The implications of this view are that acts of human destructiveness are not necessarily committed only by deranged psychopaths. Rather, a viewpoint that has come to be referred to as the "banality of evil" stresses that evil is most likely committed by very ordinary people. One biographer [G.S. Graber] of Heinrich Himmler, head of the SS [Schutzstaffel; the elite wing of the Nazi Party that administered the concentration camps], has noted that, although it is difficult to accept, we must begin to understand that many of the great monsters of history, such as Eichmann and Himmler, were not unusual examples of their culture. They were, as he characterized Himmler, "pedestrian, unimaginative—in a word, ordinary."

Similar examples of banality or ordinariness pervade the decision-making bureaucracy in the contemporary United States. For example,

Thomas K. Jones, a deputy undersecretary of defense in the Reagan administration, is quoted in Robert Scheer's book *With Enough Shovels* as saying that "the United States could fully recover from an all-out nuclear war with the Soviet Union in just two to four years." He declared that nuclear war was not nearly as devastating as we had been led to believe and went on to say, "If there are enough shovels to go around, everybody's going to make it." Scheer points out that the shovels were "for digging holes in the ground, which would be covered somehow or other with a couple of doors and three feet of dirt thrown on top, thereby providing adequate fallout shelters for the millions who had been evacuated from America's countryside." Jones claimed, "It's the dirt that does it."

How did Jones appear as he talked about nuclear destruction? Scheer describes him in a manner reminiscent of Arendt's depiction of Eichmann:

> Do not misunderstand. There was nothing deranged or hysterical about Jones' performance that night, nothing even intemperate. Jones' manner is circumspect. His house reflects a Spartan life-style. . . . His looks are cleancut, if plain, and he's trim for his forty-nine years. He seldom raises his voice and tends to speak in a drone, sometimes inaudibly. This studied, matter-of-fact style persisted even when he discussed the deaths of hundreds of millions of people, as if he were attempting by the measured tone of his voice to deny the ultimate horror of it all. I have listened many times to the tapes of this interview, and what startles me most is how easily Jones seemed to make the subject of mass death almost boring.

. . . The banality of evil, then, is clearly not confined to the Holocaust. In the nuclear era, contemporary bureaucrats were engaged in planning the destruction of the planet in a calm, almost disinterested, "almost boring," fashion. The individuals who program and play war games seem to be able to consider the possibility of mass death, involving millions of people, without realizing or caring that they are dealing with human flesh and blood. . . .

The real impact of banality is to render trivial and acceptable the most horrendous acts. When responsible individuals talk about mass death as though they were discussing the weather, they are communicating acceptance and lack of concern.

But government decision makers are not the only people engaged in these processes of justification and rationalization. Citizens on a large scale appeared unwilling to confront the reality of death by nuclear incineration. As German citizens supported and did not question Hitler's orders, U.S. citizens did not question the president's orders or even his intentions. Whatever the president does is to be supported simply because he *is* the president.

These are, of course, controversial notions because they force us to focus on our own vulnerability and to question the circumstances of our own obedience. Where, for example, does one draw the line in obeying authority? Are there different types of authority? . . . Does a person follow orders even if the ultimate result is evil? Such questions are tied closely to the third set of conditions—political conditions.

Political Conditions

Politics is tied to culture and psychology. The way people view politics and a political system and the way they learn to relate to authority are connected to what they learn as they are growing up. As children, we are all exposed to the cultural and political myths and legends common to our environment. These myths, which we learn through the process of political socialization, act as foundations upon which our adult views of the world and our adult behaviors are based.

Children learn and internalize the existing norms of their culture. If people are convinced that these norms are legitimate, that they are the accepted views of the majority, and particularly of political and social leaders, then they will obey those leaders who communicate the ideas that appear congruent with those norms. The cues that reinforce obedience are sent by people occupying important social, cultural, and political positions. If a strain of the national mythology emphasizes obedience, it is quite possible for leaders to attempt to manipulate that strain in order to convince potential participants that mass destruction is justified. Hence, if people in high positions spread dehumanizing symbolizations of another state or group of people, they send a message that it is justified to act aggressively against that state or group. Many people will always be willing to act out hostile impulses if they are reinforced by those in high positions.

During the Holocaust, the continued description of Jews as vermin and bacilli was a prime example of dehumanizing symbolization. Anti-Semitism was also reinforced by the lack of opposition to the extermination of the Jews. The fact that political and religious leaders did not object seemed to confirm the legitimacy of the destruction. The commandant of Treblinka, Franz Stangl, provided a striking example when he noted that he was profoundly affected by Cardinal Theodor Innitzer's call to Catholics to "cooperate" with the Nazis as well as by the fact that many political leaders capitulated "at once" to the Nazis. Leaders, consequently, may prepare a population for genocide in this fashion.

This process is no less true today as political figures and their advisers (reinforced by social and religious leaders) discuss war as "policy" and use terminology such as "ethnic cleansing," as in the case of the Serb massacre of the Bosnian Muslims. This form of discussion contributes to the acceptance of genocide as a desirable policy to achieve the goals of the leadership. Political leaders and their advisers thus act to legitimize genocide as an instrument of policy that is not only acceptable but also likely to be used. The state, as was the Nazi state, is turned into an executioner state as the leaders engage in the process of justification and condition the people to participate in and accept the large-scale destruction of their companions on the planet.

Understanding the Past

Obedience may thus be enhanced under three broad types of conditions. The first involves the development of cultural and racial myths and stereotypes that function to dehumanize the target population, in essence identifying the victims. Psychological conditions, the second set, require obedience to authority by individuals—that is, the people who pull the triggers and carry out the orders. The third type of conditions, political conditions, combine the giving of orders with justification of the acts of destruction. Ultimately, if we view mass murder as being carried out, at least in part, in response to these conditions, we are left with the profoundly disturbing conclusion that acts of large-scale destruction of human life may be committed by any individual or nation under the "right" cultural, psychological, or political circumstances.

Understanding the conditions that promote participation in genocide does not necessarily guarantee that these acts will not occur again. Yet we must understand the past and incorporate as an integral part of our learning experience information about genocide and mass murder so that our memory is not reconstructed by the state or those in power who may wish to convince us to kill others. How individuals respond to the language of extermination, how they react to the attempts to socialize obedience, is not predetermined.

THE GENOCIDAL IMPULSE: WHY NATIONS KILL OTHER NATIONS

Richard Morrock

Richard Morrock is vice president of the International Psychohistorical Association. In the following article, he contends that genocides arise from both psychological and historical causes stemming from a population's shared repressed emotions of anger, fear, or need. According to Morrock, individuals who repress their emotions concerning childhood traumas can become psychopathic killers. This same psychological phenomenon combined with certain economic and social conditions, he argues, can result in a nation or ethnic group willing to perform genocide. Morrock identifies three types of genocide—*instrumental, assimilative,* and *atavistic*—that are based on repressed emotions of need, fear, and anger respectively.

In her presentation to the 1998 convention of the International Psychohistorical Association (IPA), Dr. Alice Miller posed the question of why Germany, with its long history of anti-Semitism, did not instigate a Holocaust during World War I, when much of Eastern Europe was under its control. What follows is my attempt to answer that question in terms of the one major difference in the German state of mind between that war and the next: In World War II, the Germans were aware of the possibility of defeat. And in 1945, that would have meant not merely the loss of some distant colonies; rather, the Germans were led by Hitler to believe that defeat would result in the annihilation of the German nation.

There have been many cases of genocide during the twentieth century. Not all are equally familiar to Americans. The U.S. government sponsored a museum devoted to the Jewish victims of Nazi genocide, but still speaks of "allegations" of the mass murder of Armenians by the Turks, now our NATO allies. Our media blame Pol Pot for the transformation of once-peaceful Cambodia into a slaughterhouse in which 2 million people died out of 8 million; but they never hint that some of these deaths were attributable to our own client regimes, and to our massive aerial bombardment of defenseless Cambodian villages. Notwithstanding

Excerpted from Richard Morrock, "The Genocidal Impulse: Why Nations Kill Other Nations," *The Journal of Psychohistory,* Fall 1999. Reprinted with permission from *The Journal of Psychohistory.*

its sanctimonious war against Slobodan Milosevic's Serbia, the United States has long since lost the moral high ground on this issue.

Typically, genocide has been blamed by the experts on either ideology or genes. We are innocent lambs, led astray by the persuasive powers of a few evil men like Hitler or Pol Pot; or else we are killer apes, expressing nothing but our true nature when we create horrors like Auschwitz or Tuol Sleng [a prison and interrogation center in Phnom Penh, Cambodia, where thousands were tortured and killed from 1975-1979]. Let me offer a third explanation, a psychohistorical one, which does not insist that human beings are inherently dupes or demons. The genocidal impulse, I would argue, is an expression of feelings which were repressed in childhood, but remain intact in the unconscious—feelings of terror, rage, and need. When social conditions permit, these repressed feelings take the form of mass murder of officially sanctioned victims. Take away the repressed pain, and the Hitlers and Pol Pots would end up as isolated mountebanks, preaching their doctrines to nonexistent audiences; take away the historical setting that sanctions the sacrifice of entire ethnic groups, and the perpetrators would be forced to find other outlets for their urges. An explanation for genocide is not psychohistorical unless it is both psychological and historical; I am calling for trading in reductionist explanations for interactionist ones.

In good times, demagogues attract little following. This does not mean that the psychological pain they address is absent, since it typically originates in the nuclear family decades earlier; it only means that conditions are not ripe for its political expression. Millions of Americans are intensely prejudiced against blacks, and not a few still entertain murderous fantasies about Jews; but only a handful joined George Lincoln Rockwell's tiny American Nazi Party, which openly advocated violence against these two groups. Yet, had there been a serious depression during the 1960s, Rockwell's following might have increased a thousandfold. Obviously, economic collapse does not cause people to be traumatized twenty years previously, but by creating a potential threat to the system, it causes ruling elites to play the role of enablers, backing the radical right to save them from the radical left.

We must recognize the influence of childhood traumas, including birth traumas, on those who fall prey as adults to the demagogy of bloodthirsty fanatics. We must also not ignore school systems, which play a key role in socializing future members of society, sometimes traumatizing them in the bargain. Finally, we must not overlook the political and social conditions which lead to genocide. . . .

What Makes Psychopaths?

Genocide is a situation in which "ordinary Germans"—or ordinary Turks, Yugoslavs, Cambodians, or even Americans—begin to act like psychopaths. This group, who commit evil acts with the full understanding of what they are doing, have not received sufficient attention from academics or clinicians. . . . The problem is that psychopaths do not often come to the attention of clinicians, aside from a few atypical cases such as attempted presidential assassin John Hinckley, "Son of Sam" killer David Berkowitz, and homosexual cannibal Jeffrey Dahmer. Psychopaths rarely seek treatment, and most clinicians would be reluctant to take them on as patients. They don't even suffer from their past traumas; they make others suffer instead.

What we know about Dahmer and Berkowitz indicates that their crimes were not all that inexplicable. Berkowitz had been given up for adoption at birth. As a young man, stationed in Korea with the army, he took repeated doses of LSD. When he left the army, he sought out his biological mother, and they established a cordial relationship. However, when he began his killing spree, he singled out women with shoulder-length, dark hair, just like his birth mother. He might have survived the trauma of abandonment, had the LSD not blown away the remainder of his fragile defense system. The howling of a neighbor's dog triggered the feelings of loneliness and abandonment, sending Berkowitz into his murderous state.

Dahmer came from an affluent family, but his mother was a borderline psychotic. His scientist father spent little time at home. Jeffrey began to be neglected at age six, when his parents had another son. While his mother was pregnant, she let Jeffrey put his ear against her stomach to listen to the sound of his unborn brother's heartbeat. Once the younger boy was born, however, she withdrew all interest from her first child.

Dahmer was so neglected by his parents that they didn't even realize that he was an alcoholic by age twelve. When he was eighteen, his parents were on the brink of divorce, living in separate parts of the large family home. Neither bothered to inform Jeffrey when they moved out, simultaneously but separately, to get away from each other. Jeffrey woke up one day to find that the rest of his family had disappeared, leaving him with the house and no means of support. It was shortly afterward that he committed his first murder.

As a young adult, Dahmer would sometimes reenact the childhood scene with his victims, putting his ear against their stomach to listen to the sounds. His annihilation of his victims' bodies was presaged by his childhood pastime of dissolving the bodies of animals in acid, a hobby that took up much of his time. Squirrels, raccoons, and even neighborhood dogs would disappear, and he would bury their remains in his back yard. It appears that he was acting out a wish to annihilate his younger brother, so that his place as the center of his mother's attention would be restored.

The Brain's Neurotransmitters

Love and respect produce neurotransmitters in the brain, and the lack of these transmitters is correlated with increased levels of violence in experimental mice. Each of the major neurotransmitters appears to be connected with a specific mind state. Dopamine is associated with joy; norepinephrine with feelings of fear and danger; endorphine with love; and serotonin with a more indefinable set of feelings associated with status and accomplishment. Receptors in the brain take up these neurotransmitters, with different receptors acting on each of the transmitters. The relationship between the number of receptors and the amount of neurotransmitter seems to be complex, but the implication is that the particular combination of neurotransmitters in a child's brain fixes the pattern of receptors that continues into adulthood, and that the adult, if deprived of the desired level of a particular neurotransmitter, will go to great lengths to seek out experiences that produce it. Sometimes these experiences are endorsed by society; sometimes the individual has to seek out an obscure subculture; and sometimes he has to act out in an antisocial way, risking imprisonment or even death. But the need for the depleted neurotransmitter is as strong as any addict's craving for his drug.

Consequently, we have people whose norepinephrine imbalance leads them to ride roller coasters, engage in risky sports, read ghost stories, and attend every horror film released by Hollywood. Those with low endorphin levels may immerse themselves in extreme forms of conventional religion, become easy prey for "love-bombing" cults, or engage in compulsive sexual activity. Serotonin shortages may compel people to become violent criminals who thrill at the thought of holding, however briefly, life-and-death power over others; or they may become scientists or researchers eager to discover important things unknown to the rest of the world; or they may even turn into racists who convince themselves that they are inherently superior. Whatever their obvious differences, these three groups have one thing in common: they believe that they have been unfairly deprived of status.

If it is possible to explain psychological and even social events clear down to the molecular level, as I maintain here, this is not the same as holding to a reductionist paradigm, which would argue that "chemical imbalances" are the cause of disturbed behavior. What the biological reductionists consistently overlook are the *psychosocial causes* of the chemical imbalances. If the individual has too many receptors, or too little neurotransmitter, in his brain, we should not attribute this to the random act of some indifferent deity, but to threatening, abusive, neglectful, overprotective, strict, or excessively demanding child-rearing practices. Murderers—whether of individuals or entire nations—do not come out of happy homes. . . .

Three Types of Genocide

Just as individual murders differ in their causes and circumstances, so do acts of genocide. The three types of genocide I distinguish are the *instrumental,* the *assimilative,* and the *atavistic,* each of which have their roots in a particular repressed emotion.

Instrumental genocide involves the slaughter of a group of people over the issue of resources: Belgians killing Congolese in order to control the rubber and diamonds of Central Africa; French killing Algerians in order to retain the Sahara's oil fields; Japanese killing Chinese to obtain China's vast commercial markets for their cheap and shoddy (at the time) manufactured goods; or Americans killing Vietnamese so that U.S. corporations could continue to profit from their investments in the "third world" without fear of revolution. Instrumental genocide requires the least input from the perpetrators' unconscious. They are simply drafted, or hired, and sent overseas to "do a job" in the name of their country. Public opinion at home is informed that the genocide is actually a noble mission to bring "civilization," or "prosperity," or "freedom" to some benighted foreigners, who would eagerly surrender if they could only see what was good for them.

Underlying instrumental genocide is repressed *need.* While the average citizen of an imperial power stands to gain little from overseas adventures, the economic benefits that are derived from the war are misperceived as accruing to the many rather than the few. Profits, markets, and resources become symbols of whatever was withheld from us in childhood. Little wonder that affluent societies—such as France and the United States in the 1960s—found it difficult to persuade their youth to fight in their colonial wars. In contrast, eight years of costly fighting in China produced no antiwar movement in Japan. The slogan of "co-prosperity" had too strong an appeal to the common Japanese, whose standards of living were still low until the postwar era.

Assimilative genocide is the extermination of one group by another which derives from it. The victims are what I term an "origin folk." Examples of assimilative genocide would be the massacre of Hindus by Pakistani Muslims in Bangladesh, the slaughter of southern Sudanese by northerners, and the persecution of Native Americans in Central America by right-wing governments and their U.S.-trained death squads. Whereas instrumental genocide often involves killers and victims from different racial groups, assimilative genocide features warring groups sharing a common ancestry, but which evolved in different directions. The victims are those who clung to their tribal identity, while the perpetrators adopted the identity of an alien conqueror.

Assimilative genocide, psychologically, is the expression of feelings of *fear*—both of punishment and annihilation, the latter being primarily a birth memory. The stricter the childhood upbringing, the greater the likelihood that the adults will engage in such actions. The trigger is a perceived threat to the national identity—from social revolution, ethnic separatism, or annexation by a neighboring country. The greater the pain in childhood, the greater the need for identification in adult life with such broader groups as nation or religion. For those from particularly dysfunctional families, protecting the nation or the religion from enemies becomes a near-obsession. The persecution of origin-folk is isomorphic to the neurotic's repression of his real self, in order to gain the approval of others.

Buried Anger and Fear

Most dramatic of all is *atavistic genocide,* in which the perpetrators turn on a group which has played the role of a mentor. This represents the expression of buried *anger,* although fear undoubtedly plays a part as well. The classic example of atavistic genocide is the Nazi Holocaust, directed against a group of people who were held responsible for both Christianity and Marxism. The fear that the German bourgeoisie had of Marxism is understandable, in light of the left-wing revolution which nearly took power in Germany—and which did succeed briefly in Bavaria, subsequently the cradle of National Socialism. The rejection of Christianity—a more subtle process—appears to have derived from the unexpected defeat Germany suffered in World War I, during which the Germans were repeatedly told that God was on their side. The persecution of the Jews was, in part, a symbolic attack on a failed God.

Cognitive dissonance seems to play an important role in triggering atavistic genocide. People are taught certain concepts about their countries, from which they often derive unwarranted but comforting conclusions: "My country is strong; therefore I am safe," or "My country is weak; therefore I am good." When a strong country is defeated (Germany in 1918, America in 1975), it can shatter the self-image of the nation. To the extent that people's personal defenses are bound up with the national mythology, an unexpected outcome of a war can produce a markedly paranoid reaction. . .

Another example of atavistic genocide is Cambodia, where the Khmer Rouge—which had been assisted by Vietnam in its rise to power—was particularly ruthless in its persecution of the large ethnic Vietnamese minority, which played a major role in the local communist movement.

Atavistic genocide appears to be something akin to a reaction formation, in Freud's terminology. The Cambodians turned against Communism even while claiming that they were the purest of Marxist-Leninists. The Nazis were defending against their anger toward the Kaiser, who had dragged his nation into a costly and unsuccessful war—as well as toward God, who had let Germany down. German culture did not permit anger against a monarch. No king has ever been assassinated in all German history; Hitler's shocked declaration that the 1944 attempt on his life was unprecedented was no egotistical exaggeration. Rather than target their rulers, Germans historically preferred to attack the Jews instead. The legend of the "Jew Suss," which the Nazis made extensive use of in their propaganda, was based on an actual historical event. Suss was a Jewish financier who had loaned money to an unpopular king. He was murdered by nobles who couldn't bring themselves to to turn on their ruler, whom they were really angry at. The incident served as a paradigm for much of German history.

Anger was not the only repressed emotion involved in the Holocaust. The persecution of weak and defenseless groups is an expression of buried fear, and when the persecution reaches the level of genocide, the fear that motivates it is usually the fear of annihilation. Some of this comes from birth trauma, which is particularly strong in Catholic areas of Europe, where women are taught from childhood that their sexual feelings should be disowned. It should nor surprise us that Austrians were vastly overrepresented among Nazi war criminals, one historian estimating that they may have been responsible for half of all the atrocities. Severe childhood upbringing . . . can also arouse such fears, as can unexpected defeat (or victory) in war. All of these factors work together, and given so many psychological causes, it should not be surprising that the Holocaust is distinctive, even among instances of genocide, for having no rational motives.

Just as Germans in the 1930s displaced their anger against their fallen rulers toward Jewish scapegoats, so did the Khmer Rouge displace its rage against the United States toward neighboring Vietnam. But whereas the Jews were a scattered and powerless people, the Vietnamese had just defeated the world's leading superpower. It would appear that the Cambodians, raised in a society with little military tradition, were motivated far more by repressed anger than repressed fear. Members of weak nations usually do not learn to repress fear, but Cambodia's devout Buddhism was probably related to the repression of anger. Unlike the Germans, the Cambodians directed their hatred upward, against a relatively powerful target, rather than downward against a weaker one.

Common to most cases of genocide is the projection of one's own intentions onto the victims. Just as Hitler claimed that the Jews were out to rule the World, even while he planned his own world conquest, so did the Cambodians attribute expansionist ambitions to Vietnam, although it was the Khmer Rouge which actually sought to annex territory from its neighbors. There is a parallel with serial killer John Wayne Gacy, who projected his own despised qualities onto his young male victims before killing them.

The Persistence
of Human Brutality

Nicholas Baldoni

In 1999, Serbian forces attacked ethnic Albanians in the province of Kosovo, killing hundreds and leaving thousands homeless. Nicholas Baldoni, a freelance writer specializing in human rights issues, states in the following essay that Kosovo is but the latest example of humanity's tendency to commit genocidal acts. Despite modern ideals of civilized behavior and the protection of human rights, Baldoni contends, many people still believe that ethnic violence and genocide are viable solutions to political problems. The answer to the disturbing question of why genocides have occurred throughout history, he suggests, may lie in the existence of a tragic moral flaw within humanity, one that in certain circumstances allows people to become killers.

The moral crisis in the Serbian province of Kosovo has once again forced the international community to confront the seemingly inextinguishable thirst in the heart of humanity for violence. Mass murder, despite the many reminders we leave for ourselves by preserving the empty furnaces at places like Auschwitz and Buchenwald, still seems to be regarded as a viable alternative, transcending ethnic and racial boundaries. Though outrage on an international scale tends to follow the discovery (whether latent or immediate) of such acts, one always feels that an act of true evil must be coupled with some other interest—economic or political—in order to truly gain the undivided attention of the international community.

As with history in general, personal biases and agendas play a crucial role in what is emphasized and ignored. Tibet exemplifies this point perfectly. The destruction of Tibetan culture and the killing of the Tibetan people was evident long before Hollywood decided to make it a popular issue; and though a certain degree of altruism may have supplied a fraction of Hollywood's motivation, its main impetus was plainly economic. If Kosovo were as remote as Tibet, in terms of geographic proximity and political interest, would the United States and the rest of the world be as interested? The answer is probably not.

Reprinted from Nicholas Baldoni, "Kosovo: The Status of Human Brutality," *The Humanist,* May/June 1999. Reprinted with permission from the author.

In short, moral outrage alone is generally not enough to inspire action on the part of the powers that be.

Precedents such as these are dangerous. Uniting the value of human life with its current political and economic worth serves to only devalue the importance of human life in general. Tying morality to money and leverage cheapens life and allows those in power to ignore terrible human rights violations—or even commit them—in order to secure an economic or political end.

Ethnic Slaughter

The situation in Kosovo offers an example of the most serious form of human rights abuse: ethnic slaughter. History is riddled with examples of this kind: the pogroms of the Middle Ages designed to destroy the effect and presence of Jewish culture in "Christian Europe"; the policy of removal of Native Americans brought to maturity by Andrew Jackson; the entire institution of slavery, which served to denigrate an entire race of people to the status of livestock. The gross evil unleashed upon the world by the Nazis, though by far the most popular example of genocide, is still contested by those who believe it to be a hoax. And though those who believe in such propaganda are usually relegated to irrelevance in most quarters, the example of Hitler proves that those previously considered pathetic and irrational can overcome mainstream sensibilities and twist them according to their own purposes. Even in the 1990s, vast human rights violations and acts of ethnic slaughter—embodied in the killings in Bosnia-Herzegovina and the inexcusable bloodshed in the African nations of Uganda and Rwanda—have come to poison our current legacy.

In many ways, humanity has excelled in attitudes and methods of mass persecution and murder. The question, then, is not whether acts of ethnic persecution and genocide will happen again, since the record of history has proven them to be irrepressible. Instead, the question is why do they continue to haunt humankind throughout history?

Humanity's Tragic Flaw

The answer seems to lie in the presumed dark side of humanity—the temple of brutality, which loses its vague aura of presumption with every new report of ethnic slaughter, such as those now occurring in Kosovo. Human barbarism seems to transcend the passage of time so thoroughly that even vast changes in our fundamental belief systems have left it unchanged. The church-sponsored pogroms of the Middle Ages, though inexcusable from any and all vantage points, were in some ways the symptom of archaic dogma, which at least served as a catalyst for humanity's sleeping potential for violence.

However, the same cannot be said for humanity in the modern era. Unlike our historical predecessors, twentieth-century humanity has well-developed concepts of human rights, democracy, and egalitarian social responsibility, and yet we still descend into the same pit of mass death and persecution, as if viciousness and death lingered on the periphery of human existence waiting to explode into the open. In fact, the argument could be made that the current moral state of humanity has actually decayed since the early part of the millennium, in light of humankind's greater degree of knowledge concerning what is right and wrong.

Ultimately, one is forced to confront the possibility of a tragic flaw existing in the heart of all humanity—the idea that at any time, given the right set of circumstances, one can be stripped of the clothes of civilization and moral responsibility and run brutal and naked into the forest of human barbarism.

CHAPTER 3

GENOCIDE: PREVENTION AND PUNISHMENT

THE FAILURE OF THE INTERNATIONAL COMMUNITY TO PREVENT OR PUNISH GENOCIDE

Diane F. Orentlicher

Diane F. Orentlicher is a professor of law and the director of the War Crimes Research Office at the Washington College of Law at American University, Washington, D.C. She has written several books on human rights and international law, including *Genocide and Crimes Against Humanity: The Legal Regime.* In the following essay, Orentlicher describes what she sees as the global communi-ty's failure to enforce the Convention on the Prevention and Punishment of the Crime of Genocide, adopted by the United Nations in 1948. She argues that although the convention "has come to embody the conscience of humanity," the record of actual enforcement is poor since most nations have chosen to ignore or discount probable cases of genocide.

Invoked with a frequency, familiarity, and reverence rarely associated with instruments of law, the 1948 Convention on the Prevention and Punishment of the Crime of Genocide has come to embody the con-science of humanity.

Its moral force is surely ironic. For the record of the Genocide Con-vention since its adoption has been notable above all for States' nearly wholesale failure to enforce its terms.

Although the treaty envisages (but does not require) the creation of an international court to punish genocide, forty-five years passed before the first international criminal tribunal was established. Its jurisdiction was limited to crimes, including genocide, committed in the former Yugoslavia since 1991. A similar, more circumscribed, tri-bunal was created for Rwanda one year later. It was not until Septem-ber 2, 1998—a half-century after the United Nations General Assembly adopted the Genocide Convention—that the first verdict interpreting the convention was rendered by an international tribunal following a trial (one other defendant had previously pleaded guilty to genocide). On that day the Rwanda Tribunal found Jean-Paul Akayesu guilty on nine counts for his role in the 1994 Rwandan genocide.

Reprinted from Diane F. Orentlicher, "Genocide," in *Crimes of War: What the Public Should Know,* edited by Roy Gutman and David Rieff. Copyright © 1999 Crimes of War Project. Reprinted with permission from W.W. Norton & Company, Inc.

Nor did any State bring a case under the Genocide Convention to the World Court until 1993, and this was scarcely a milestone in international enforcement efforts. The case was brought by a State that had endured genocidal crimes—Bosnia-Herzegovina—against a State allegedly responsible—the former Yugoslavia—and not by other States determined to enforce the law of universal conscience on behalf of desperate victims beyond their borders.

To the contrary, when those same crimes were being committed—and gruesomely portrayed in the daily media—legal experts in the U.S. government were asked, in the words of a former State Department lawyer, "to perform legal gymnastics to avoid calling this genocide." And as Rwandan Hutus slaughtered hundreds of thousands of Tutsis, the Clinton administration instructed its spokespeople not to describe what was happening as genocide lest this "inflame public calls for action," according to the *New York Times*. Instead, the State Department and National Security Council reportedly drafted guidelines instructing government spokespeople to say that "acts of genocide may have occurred" in Rwanda.

Five decades of nonenforcement have left the Genocide Convention's core terms shrouded in considerable ambiguity, making it that much easier for recalcitrant politicians to equivocate. (Such equivocations nonetheless fly in the face of the convention, which requires States parties not only to punish genocide—a measure that does demand legal certainty—but also to prevent and repress the crime—action that by its nature must not await the certain knowledge that genocide has occurred.)

Defining Genocide

The definition of genocide set forth in the Genocide Convention is authoritative and has been incorporated verbatim in the statutes of the Yugoslavia and Rwanda tribunals as well as that of a permanent International Criminal Court (ICC) that will be created after sixty states have ratified the statute adopted in Rome in July 1998. After affirming that genocide is a crime under international law whether committed in time of peace or war, the 1948 convention defines genocide as "any of the following acts committed with intent to destroy, in whole or in part, a national, ethnical, racial or religious group, as such: killing members of the group; causing serious bodily or mental harm to members of the group; deliberately inflicting on the group conditions of life calculated to bring about its physical destruction in whole or in part; imposing measures intended to prevent births within the group; forcibly transferring children of the group to another group."

In the 1948 convention, then, the crime of genocide has both a physical element—comprising certain enumerated acts, such as killing members of a racial group—and a mental element—those acts must have been committed with the intent to destroy, in whole or in part, a national, ethnic, racial, or religious group "as such." In its verdict in the Akayesu case, the Rwanda Tribunal found that the systematic rape of Tutsi women in Taba Province constituted the genocidal act of "causing serious bodily or mental harm to members of the [targeted] group."

In addition to the crime of genocide itself, the 1948 convention provides that the following acts shall be punishable: conspiracy to commit genocide, direct and public incitement to commit genocide, attempt to commit genocide, and complicity in genocide.

What was left out of the convention is as important as what was included. Although earlier drafts of the convention listed political groups among those covered by the intent requirement, this category was omitted during final drafting stages. Too many governments, it seemed, would be vulnerable to the charge of genocide if deliberate destruction of political groups fell within the crime's compass.

Also excluded was the concept of cultural genocide—destroying a group through forcible assimilation into the dominant culture. The drafting history makes clear that the 1948 convention was meant to cover physical destruction of a people; the sole echo of efforts to include the notion of cultural extermination is the convention's reference to forcibly transferring children of a targeted group to another group.

In this and other respects the conventional definition of genocide is narrower than the conception of Polish scholar Raphael Lemkin, who first proposed at an international conference in 1933 that a treaty be created to make attacks on national, religious, and ethnic groups an international crime. Lemkin, who served in the U.S. War Department, fashioned the term genocide from the Greek word genos, meaning race or tribe, and the Latin term for killing, cide. (In his 1944 book, *Axis Rule in Occupied Europe,* Lemkin noted that the same idea could also come from the term "ethnocide, consisting of the Greek word 'ethnos'—nation—and the Latin word 'cide.' ")

Although Lemkin's conception included the physical extermination of targeted groups, this was, in his view, only the most extreme technique of genocide:

> By "genocide" we mean the destruction of an ethnic group . . . . Generally speaking, genocide does not necessarily mean the immediate destruction of a nation, except when accomplished by mass killings of all members of a nation. It is intended rather to signify a coordinated plan of different actions aiming at the destruction of essential foundations of the life of national groups, with the aim of annihilating the groups themselves. The objectives of such a plan would be disintegration of the political and social institutions, of culture, language, national feelings, religion, and the economic existence of national

groups, and the destruction of the personal security, liberty, health, dignity, and even the lives of the individuals belonging to such groups. . . .

Genocide has two phases: one, destruction of the national pattern of the oppressed group; the other, the imposition of the national pattern of the oppressor. This imposition, in turn, may be made upon the oppressed population which is allowed to remain, or upon the territory alone, after removal of the population and colonization of the area by the oppressor's own nationals.

Four years would pass before Lemkin's crime was recognized in an international treaty, but the legal foundation was laid during the 1945 Nuremberg and other postwar prosecutions. Although the Nuremberg Charter did not use the term genocide, its definition of crimes against humanity overlapped significantly with Lemkin's conception of genocide. The term genocide was used in the indictment against major war criminals tried at Nuremberg, who were accused of having "conducted deliberate and systematic genocide, viz., the extermination of racial and national groups, against the civilian populations of certain occupied territories in order to destroy particular races and classes of people and national, racial or religious groups." Nuremberg prosecutors also invoked the term in their closing arguments, and it also appeared in the judgments of several U.S. military tribunals operating in Nuremberg.

Shortly after the trial of major war criminals at Nuremberg, the UN General Assembly adopted a resolution affirming that genocide is a "crime under international law." In its preamble, the 1946 resolution termed genocide "a denial of the right of existence of entire human groups, as homicide is the denial of the right to live of individual human beings."

Questions of Intent and Responsibility

The comparatively narrow terms of the 1948 convention—in particular, its exclusion of political groups and its restrictive intent requirement—have enabled political leaders to raise doubts about whether probable genocides satisfy the convention's stringent criteria. Did the authors of the Anfal campaigns of 1988 [during which the Iraqi military attacked Kurdish villages with chemical weapons], in which at least fifty thousand Iraqi Kurds are estimated to have been massacred, intend to kill Kurds "as such" or, in the words of one leading scholar, was their aim to eliminate "the Kurdish movement as a political problem?" Did Serb perpetrators of ethnic cleansing in Bosnia intend to destroy Muslims and Croats "as such," or did they "merely" seek to establish homogeneous Serb control over coveted territory?

As these questions suggest, a key source of ambiguity is the meaning of the 1948 convention's intent requirement. Although the drafting history is somewhat ambiguous, I believe that it is a mistake to treat the convention's use of the term intent as though it were synonymous with motive. That Serb perpetrators of ethnic cleansing may have slaughtered Muslims so that they could obtain control over territory does not negate their intent to destroy Muslims "as such" in order to achieve their ultimate goal.

The Genocide Convention imposes a general duty on States parties "to prevent and to punish" genocide. Those charged with genocide are to be tried either in the State where the crime occurred or "by such international penal tribunal as may have jurisdiction with respect to those Contracting Parties which shall have accepted its jurisdiction." Although the convention does not mention a third possibility—prosecution in a third State—it is now well established that any State can assert jurisdiction over crimes of genocide, wherever the crimes occurred and whatever the nationality of the perpetrators and victims.

In addition to individual criminal responsibility for genocide, the convention also establishes State responsibility—that is, international legal responsibility of the State itself for breaching its obligations under the convention. Parties to the convention can bring a case before the International Court of Justice alleging that another State party is responsible for genocide. As noted above, the first case of this sort was brought against Yugoslavia by Bosnia-Herzegovina in 1993 and is still pending.

Article 8 of the convention contemplates measures not only to punish genocide, but also to stop it in its tracks: "Any Contracting Party may call upon the competent organs of the United Nations to take such action under the Charter of the United Nations as they consider appropriate for the prevention and suppression of acts of genocide or any of the other acts enumerated in article 3." States that are parties to the convention could, for example, seek Security Council authorization to use military force to stop genocide being committed in another country.

Finally, although treaties themselves are binding only on States that are parties to the treaties, in a 1951 advisory opinion the International Court of Justice observed that the principles underlying the Genocide Convention are part of customary international law, which binds all states.

Genocide in History

Although Lemkin implied that Nazi crimes were fundamentally different from any previously committed, Hitler's "Final Solution" was not the first campaign of extermination that would meet Lemkin's definition of genocide. The systematic extermination of Armenians by the Young Turks beginning in April 1915 was the first genocide in the twentieth century. Emboldened by the world's acquiescence in the slaughter of Armenians—over 1 million are estimated to have been put to death—Hitler is famously reported to have reassured doubters in his ranks by asking, "Who after all is today speaking of the Armenians?"

Among more recent episodes of wholesale slaughter, at least some scholars have concluded that the Turkish massacre of Kurds in the district of Dersim in 1937–1938, the massacre of Hutus by Tutsi perpetrators in Burundi in 1972, the Khmer Rouge campaign of extermination [in Cambodia] in the mid-1970s, and the 1988 Anfal campaign against Iraqi Kurds meet the legal definition of genocide.

Among these cases, perhaps none better illustrates the complexities of the 1948 convention's definition of genocide than the case of Cambodia. In view of the magnitude of the carnage there—1.5 million out of Cambodia's 7 million citizens are believed to have died as a result of Khmer Rouge policies—there has been a keen desire to affix the term genocide to their crimes. Since, however, both the perpetrators and the majority of victims were Khmer, reaching this conclusion has required agile legal reasoning. Some scholars have invoked the concept of auto-genocide, arguing that it is possible to satisfy the 1948 convention's definition even when the perpetrators sought to kill a substantial portion of their own ethnic/national group. Others, more conservatively, have conceded that the vast majority of victims were killed for reasons that may be broadly termed political, but note that certain minority groups, such as the Muslim Cham and Khmer Buddhists, were specially targeted for destruction and argue that at least the crimes against these groups were genocidal.

While some campaigns of extermination more clearly qualify as genocide than others—the Holocaust and the 1994 Rwandan genocide are instances—the truth is that plausible arguments can be raised with respect to most cases of possible genocide. In the absence of judicial resolution or political resolve, virtually any case of genocide can be questioned. The first defendant tried before the Rwanda Tribunal argued, for example, that the massacres in Rwanda were politically motivated, a gruesome manner of waging civil war. In response the tribunal concluded that, "alongside the conflict . . . genocide was committed in Rwanda in 1994 against the Tutsi as a group." That the execution of this genocide "was probably facilitated by the conflict" did not negate the fact that genocide occurred.

The dearth of precedents enforcing the convention—a grim testament to the international community's failure of will—has for decades left experts able to do little more than argue knowledgeably about whether well-known candidates for the label "genocide" meet the legal definition. The ambiguities built into the Genocide Convention can finally be resolved only when States are willing to acknowledge forthrightly that genocide has occurred and to enforce the law of conscience.

THE NEED FOR A PERMANENT INTERNATIONAL CRIMINAL COURT

Howard Ball

Many people involved in the creation of the United Nations Genocide Convention in 1948 envisaged the formation of a permanent international criminal court (ICC) to enforce its provisions. However, it was not until July 1998 that nations meeting in Rome, Italy, agreed to a treaty creating such a court with the power to prosecute perpetrators of genocide. (Temporary international tribunals had already been formed to investigate and punish acts of genocide in Rwanda and the former Yugoslavia.) The United States participated in the Rome discussions but refused to endorse the treaty. The following essay by Howard Ball, a political science professor at the University of Vermont, examines the arguments made by the court's supporters and opponents. Ball concludes that a permanent ICC would ensure that genocide would not go unpunished.

The paradox of the twentieth century is that although it has been prolific in terms of producing international treaties that define and codify war crimes, crimes against humanity, and genocide, it has evidenced a kind of brutality never before experienced in the violent history of the world. The treaties were efforts to diminish the evils of civil, regional, and world wars. Yet the bestiality evidenced in the wars of the twentieth century absolutely stunned, again and again, the world's conscience. The post–World War II war crimes trials at Nuremberg and Tokyo were an international response to the genocides discovered by the victors.

Does the adoption and certain ratification of the Rome statute of the International Criminal Court (ICC) by at least sixty nation-states by December 31, 2000, close the circle that began with the creation of the Nuremberg International Military Tribunal (IMT)? Without major power support, the question is whether it will be an *effective* international criminal tribunal. And an answer will be forthcoming the next time a Hitler or a Karadzic or a Milosevic or a Pol Pot emerges from the depths and seizes power.

Is the unfinished legacy of the World War II trials of Nazi Germany's and Japan's major war criminals finally finished? After the war ended in 1945, the victorious Allies vowed that the unimaginable atrocities committed by the Nazis and the Japanese would never occur again. . . .

Individual responsibility for planning and implementing "final solutions" for Jews, Gypsies, Russians, Chinese, and other targeted "demonized" groups was acknowledged in international law in 1945. Generals, admirals, and government leaders were brought to the dock of justice to face allegations that they were involved in unhuman and criminal actions. The concepts of "sovereign immunity," "military necessity," and "following a superior's orders" were of little help to the defendants in the post–World War II trials. Tyranny and savage behavior were on trial, and they lost. In the end, the individual was held responsible in international law for his actions against others, either in peacetime or during war.

Two Obstacles to an Effective ICC

The hope after Nuremberg and Tokyo was that the international criminal laws that emerged from the ashes of the killing centers would become effective deterrents against any new Hitlers that might emerge. The unfulfilled hope, after these trials, was that there would be a permanent court and an independent prosecutor that would effectively act against the world's new tyrants, apprehending, trying, and punishing them in a permanent ICC.

The world is on the verge of seeing such a permanent ICC become a reality. However, its success is problematic for two basic reasons. One of the essential questions is whether it will ever get off the ground, given the opposition by the United States (and other major world powers). Can the ICC be an effective deterrent without the most powerful nation in the world prepared to use its influence and its military power to ensure the court's success? An ICC *must* be supported—at least financially and militarily—by the major powers sitting on the Security Council. (As seen with the International Criminal Tribunal, Yugoslavia (ICTY) and the International Criminal Tribunal, Rwanda (ICTR), finding the human resources to staff and support the prosecutor's office and the court bureaucracy is going to be an immense problem, and it will be almost impossible if funding from the major powers is not forthcoming.)

The second question begging for an answer is, What can an international criminal tribunal possibly do to lessen the wanton, unbelievable cruelty the world's population has seen inflicted on tens of millions of civilians in the twentieth century? Can the ICC punish those who commit such horrendous crimes, and will its actions deter future genocides?

Explaining the Cruelty

Scholars, political leaders, military leaders, ethicists, and religious leaders, among others, have struggled to explain the cruelty exhibited by one group against another group: the Hutu genocide of Tutsi, the Khmer Rouge annihilation of the Buddhists, the genocide committed by Bosnian Serbs against their erstwile friends and neighbors the Bosnian Muslims, the Nazi slaughter of Jews, and so on. Since Nuremberg and Tokyo, there have been at least fifteen major genocides:

USSR, 1943–1947 (ethnic minorities)
China, 1950–1951 (landlords)
Tibet, 1951 (Buddhists)
Sudan, 1955–1972 (nationalists)
Indonesia, 1965–1966 (Communists)
China, 1966–1975 (Cultural Revolution victims)
Uganda, 1971–1979 (opponents of Idi Amin)
Pakistan, 1971 (Bengali nationalists)
Cambodia, 1975–1979 ("new people" and ethnic and religious minorities)
Afghanistan, 1978–1989 (political opponents)
Sudan, 1983–1998 (nationalists)
Iraq, 1984–1991 (Kurds)
Yugoslavia, 1991–1995 (Bosnian Muslims and Croats); 1998–(Kosovars)
Burundi, 1993–1998 (Tutsi)
Rwanda, 1994 (Tutsi)

Approximately 15 million persons, mostly civilian, were massacred during these incidents. Chile, under military dictator Pinochet (1973–1990), was another nation where thousands of persons, including Spanish and French citizens residing in Chile, "disappeared," never to be seen alive again. Such disappearances also happened in Argentina and in Guatemala, where indigenous villages were destroyed with the accompanying murders of over 200,000 innocent Guatemalan men, women, and children.

As contemporary essayist Lance Morrow wrote recently:

The genocidal impulses that led the Hutu to slaughter one million Tutsi in 1994 are identical to the tribal bloodlusts at work in the Balkans. Eerily the same: the neighbors who suddenly turn a killing fury upon neighbors, the roving bands fueled round the clock on alcohol, the strange, dull light in the murderers' eyes, the sudden civic duty to exterminate the Other.

Why Ordinary People Kill

How could "ordinary men," persons who had lived with and alongside those they massacred, commit such unimaginable crimes? How could they, using the euphemisms of genocide, "clear the brush," engage in "ethnic cleansing," engage in "collective work," or implement the "final solution"? How could they come to believe and then to say to their enemy, before killing her, that she was:

> to be murdered because "to allow you to live is no benefit, to destroy you is no loss" (Cambodia)
> an "undesirable parasite" (Bosnia)
> a rodent, or vermin, or a disease carrier (all)
> "less valuable than a pig, because a pig is edible" (Japan)
> "a sleazy cockroach" (Rwanda–Hutu Power)
> "unworthy of life" (Nazi Germany)
> "dog food" (Turkey)
> wearing glasses (Cambodia)
> "less than nothing" (Nazi Germany)
> the people's "vampire" (Nazi Germany)
> a creature not of this world, with horns and tails (Rwanda–Hutu Power)
> subhuman, and her murder "would create no greater moral weight than squashing a bug or butchering a hog" (Japan)

The answer to why ordinary men kill innocent civilians so barbarically is a multifaceted one. Genocide is, in part, one's response to the brutalization of war, or deference to authority, or obedience to orders, or just plain racism. For author Christopher Browning, two factors stand apart from the rest: ideological indoctrination and propaganda, and the concept of "distancing," a corollary of the first.

Indoctrination of the ordinary men and women who committed the crimes against humanity began before the genocide began, whether in Nazi Germany, Japan, Cambodia, Bosnia, or Rwanda. In all these genocidal societies, there were training programs to imbue the cadres and the ordinary people with racist hatred of the Jew or the Chinese, of the bourgeoisie in Cambodia or the Muslims and Croats in Bosnia, of the Tutsi in Rwanda. And ordinary men, for the most part, went along with the racist propaganda because they needed to conform to the norms of the group (of killers) and of the state.

The second factor that explains the killing fields since 1915 is the dehumanization, the demonization, of selected groups—political, religious, ethnic—that the regime wanted to disappear from the face of the earth. In a perversion of Aristotle's "equals treated equally; unequals treated unequally," the racial ideology of the regime, presented to ordinary men in the press, in posters, on the radio, and in film and plays, created a demon—without any human characteristics—in the minds of the loyal, conforming citizens. . . .

Browning also maintains, after studying a group of over 100 middle-aged men from Hanover, Germany, who were used by the Nazis to kill Jews rounded up in Poland, that the "distancing [factor] is one of the keys to explaining why ordinary men kill."

When an enemy is successfully denied humanity (through the propaganda and indoctrination of the ordinary men and women of the regime), he becomes what the labels say he is: less than human. When members of the targeted group are called *untermenschen* or cockroach again and again, ordinary men eventually come to regard them as worthless. Recall the Khmer Rouge soldier who told a few professionals that "to save you is no benefit, to kill you is no loss to Angkar."

For most of these soldiers and killing units, there was no problem in doing away with, murdering, these innocent people. Jews, Buddhist monks, and Tutsis were not the equal of Hitler's SS, the Khmer Rouge, or the Hutu killing units. Noted historian Raul Hilberg observed that the Nazi destruction of Jews was based on three premises: (1) no Jew was overlooked in the effort to destroy the whole cohort, (2) "the complex relationship between Jews and non-Jews was to be severed with least harm to individual Germans and to the economy as a whole," and (3) "the killings had to be conducted in a manner that would limit psychological repercussions in the ranks of the perpetrators, prevent unrest among the victims, and preclude anxiety or protest in the non-Jewish population." This pattern of behavior was seen in Bosnia, Rwanda, and Cambodia and in the Kosovo madness.

In all these genocides, there was the specter of what Nigerian playwright Wole Soyinka calls "unrepentant participation" by the overwhelming majority of ordinary men and women. In light of this reality, what can international law do to minimize such behavior on the part of the leaders as well as the rank-and-file killers of innocent civilians who have been demonized, dehumanized, and damned with the label "the Other"? Can anything be done by international organizations such as the ICC to address this problem, thereby deterring future genocides? This question is almost impossible to answer. The answer, ultimately, rests with society's leaders.

A Comparison: Nuremberg and the ICC

What do the Nuremberg IMT and the ICC have in common? Did the Nuremberg trial address the demonization issue? Will the ICC be able to apprehend, arrest, try, and convict those who have committed genocide?

First of all, the ICC is a permanent criminal court, with jurisdiction to hear cases involving grievous acts including war crimes, crimes against humanity, genocide, and carrying on an aggressive war. The Nuremberg IMT was an ad hoc tribunal and ceased to exist after the judgment and verdicts were read in 1946. Also, the ICC's Chamber will consist of judges elected by all the member nations in the UN General Assembly that have ratified the Rome statute. The Nuremberg tribunal consisted of judges from the four victorious Allies.

For some, such as John R. Bolton, former assistant secretary of state for international organizational affairs, there is no analogy. Nuremberg

was a "victors' tribunal," where the probable defendants were in custody and the "whole of the German archives was available and was
seized by the victorious allies upon the total surrender of the Nazis
and Japanese." Alfred P. Rubin, international law professor at the
Fletcher School of Law and Diplomacy at Tufts University, supports
Bolton's contentions.

Furthermore, the defeated axis powers were occupied by the victorious armies of the United Nations. Thousands of Nazis (and Japanese)
leaders and followers who were alleged to have committed war crimes
and crimes against humanity were apprehended and brought to trial
before Allied judges—French, British, Russian, and American jurists
assigned to preside over these lesser-known trials that took place in
the four occupied zones of Berlin and in Allied courts in the Pacific
Rim. The major war criminals were sent to Nuremberg to stand trial
for their war crimes.

In both the Nuremberg and the Tokyo war crimes tribunals, there
was clear evidence of the bureaucratization of genocide. In Cambodia,
Bosnia, and Rwanda, there was a decision-making entity, called Angkar
or Hutu Power or Milosevic, that issued general orders to kill the enemy
and gave the killers free rein regarding the manner of massacre. Most of
the killers lived next to or knew the innocents they killed. It was common to hear horrible tales from survivors of the mass killings; for
example, that two of the many men who had raped a victim were her
high school teachers. However, although friends and neighbors of the
victims did much of the killing, there was also the presence of a
bureaucracy that informed and directed the killers. Wole Soyinka
recalled one such example of bureaucratic genocide in Rwanda:

> [A Hutu *bourgmestre*] felt personally indicted after a visit from
> a Government official, who accused the citizenry of being lax
> in the task of "bush clearing"—one of the many euphemisms
> for the task of eliminating the Tutsi. A day after the official
> departed, the [mayor], whose wife was a Tutsi, called a meet-
> ing of the villagers for some soul-searching. He took his four
> sons with him. He began his address by revealing that, having
> taken to heart the rebuke from their visitor, he had decided to
> set an example, and thus slaughtered his Tutsi wife before
> leaving home. But that was only the first step, he said. It was
> not enough to kill all Tutsi, they must eliminate every vestige
> of Tutsi blood that contaminated the purity of the breed. . . .
> And with one stroke of his machete, he lopped off the head of
> his eldest son. One by one, three other sons were led out of
> the hut in which he kept them, and slaughtered. And with
> that, another village that, until then, had withstood the hate
> rhetoric of the *interahamwe* dived headfirst into the sump of
> bloodletting.

The ICTY and the ICTR, unlike the Nuremberg and Tokyo trials, were the right deeds done for the wrong reason, according to human rights activist Aryeh Neier. These tribunals were created as "substitutes for effective action [by the UN and the major powers] to halt Serb [and Hutu] depredations in BiH [Bosnia-Herzegovina] [and Rwanda]." The major powers, especially the United States, shamefully evaded action to prevent and then to end the genocides in Bosnia and Rwanda. *Time* essayist Lance Morrow writes that "Madeleine Albright, who was Clinton's ambassador to the UN, temporized as the death toll in Rwanda climbed into the hundreds of thousands. It was 'the absolute low point of her career as a statesperson.'" Even after the Dayton Peace Accord was signed, albeit reluctantly by the Bosnian Serbs, the North Atlantic Treaty Organization (NATO) powers and the UN put the minimum number of troops into the region and developed operational plans that avoided potential hot spots where fighting could take place between Implementation Force (IFOR) soldiers and Bosnian Serb fighters.

In Yugoslavia, where 60,000 NATO and UN troops have been patrolling BiH since 1996, Radovan Karadzic and Ratko Mladic, the two major leaders of the Bosnian Serbs, are still fugitives from the ICTY. (General Mladic retired comfortably in Belgrade, Serbia, on his army pension; Karadzic is somewhere in Republika Srpska, moving regularly to avoid capture by NATO forces patrolling BiH.) There has been little effort to apprehend such fugitives because of fears of bloodshed.

In Rwanda, many of the Hutu military leaders have found safe haven in bordering nation-states. From these locations, they have led military raids into Rwanda, killing tens of thousands of Tutsi and moderate Hutu.

This suggests another basic difference between the 1945 and the 1998 tribunals: in 1945, the defendants were in custody; today, there is no mechanism for searching for and seizing persons who have been indicted. If a nation's military plays the role of bounty hunter, the fear is that there will be military attacks on the troops trying to apprehend those indicted by the ICC.

The Justice of the Matter

Justice for victims of genocide and other war crimes is achieved when the alleged war criminal is in the dock or, preferably, dead. Can there be a stable peace in Rwanda, Bosnia, Cambodia, and other countries that have experienced genocide and crimes against humanity if the perpetrators do not stand trial? Can there be peace without that type of justice?

There is a delicate balance that must be struck between peace and justice. Clearly, in world politics, as seen most recently in the 1995 Dayton Peace Accord, realpolitik dictates that peace is, on balance, more valuable than providing justice for the victims of war crimes and genocide. At Dayton, the idea of using IFOR troops to hunt for defendants, arrest them, and transport them to the Hague for trial was rejected. At Dayton, Slobodan Milosevic, the major architect of the "ethnic cleansing" program, as well as the supplier of arms and equipment to the Bosnian Serbs, sat around the conference table with other national leaders.

There are others who argue that providing justice will ease the way to peace in a nation devastated by war. Trying war criminals furthers the goal of justice in three ways. In a trial before an ICC:

1. There is the assignment of specific, individual guilt, thereby avoiding collective guilt.
2. There is the acknowledgment of the victims of the genocide.
3. There is established, in the words of Marshall Harris et al., "an accurate historical record of the nature of and responsibility for the crimes committed."

For many, the last justification is the most important one. Roger Rosenblatt wrote that the struggle of men against power is the struggle of memory over forgetting. If there are no ICC trials of alleged war criminals, there will be no accurate memory. Without the thousands of pages of documents and tribunal judgments, the victims' suffering and the horrid deeds of the killers will in part rest in the hands of the "revisionists," persons who say that the Jewish Holocaust never occurred. And the perpetrators will have accomplished one of their goals: to erase all memory of the victims.

There is also an urgent need for justice for the hundreds of thousands of civilians in Cambodia, BiH, Rwanda, and Kosovo who have become reluctant displaced persons. . . .

American Objections

Since Secretary of State Robert Lansing objected to the creation of a permanent international criminal court to try the kaiser and other German military and civilian leaders for war crimes at Versailles in 1919, U.S. policy has remained the same. The U.S. government has objected to and voted against any international organization that would weaken the concept of sovereign immunity. Examination of UN Ambassador Bill Richardson's speeches, or the comments of David Scheffer, head of the U.S. delegation to the Rome conference, places the observer in a time warp back to 1919.

For the Americans and others at Versailles and at Rome, the twentieth century was a century of nation-state dominance. There would never be acceptance of an international treaty that threatened American citizens, especially U.S. military forces. From the record at Rome and a number of speeches given by American policy makers and military leaders afterward, as well as the loud outbursts of defiance from Senator Jesse Helms, it seems that either the Rome statute must be amended or the United States must eventually sign the protocol, with its reservations noted as a matter of international law. . . .

The ICC and Human Nature

Can belligerents be constrained by the rule of law in their actions on the battlefield and toward civilians in occupied territory? If not, then the presence of an ICC is necessary to deny impunity to the killers. Is human nature affected by international conventions such as the Nuremberg Principles and the Genocide Convention? Will these international laws serve as deterrents to the commission of war crimes and genocide in the future? Or are they, as Nazi War criminal Hermann Göring cynically said, "mere toilet paper"?

In the movement toward a permanent ICC that began eight decades ago, there are two opposing camps. Both base their comments about the effectiveness of an ICC on different views of human nature. One group, the realist school of foreign policy, denies the efficacy of international law and, by implication, places limits on the effectiveness of both domestic and international law. This argument is premised on a negative, base view of human nature. Adherents argue . . . that human beings are false, ever quarreling, and warlike and readily use force and extreme cruelty against their enemies to achieve domestic and foreign policy goals. International legal restraints on their behavior hardly matter; the only restraint that is effective in deterring genocidal behavior is the use of force against them. And the only effective military force, at the end of the twentieth century, is the armed might of a small number of powerful nation-states. . . .

Critics of the ICC created in Rome in July 1998, including members of the Clinton administration, have proffered this realistic (read cynical) view of human nature. The Security Council, argued the U.S. delegates, must play a substantive role in the activities of a successful ICC because it has the ability to use force to buttress ICC opinions. This position also gives the five permanent members of the Security Council a veto power over possible ICC actions.

Without such involvement by the major world powers, the ICC would be impotent. To alienate a world power such as the United States at the Rome conference was to possibly minimize its role as military enforcer of ICC orders and judgments. And without the use of force by the UN in its peace-keeping operations, there is no peace.

Furthermore, the realists claim that law has little or no impact on human behavior. . . .

The other camp has a less pessimistic view of human nature. . . . They maintain that law can have an impact on humans because they are capable of doing righteous deeds and will do acts of loving-kindness for other less fortunate human beings. In their view, law is a "lodestar," a target that fallible human beings hope to reach someday. Brightly lighting up the sky and showing humans the proper direction for both individual and community actions, this notion of law implies that human nature can be positively impacted by treaties and their messages about the limits of human behavior. Unlike the realists, they see nation-states sharing common interests, such as punishing those who commit genocide, that are advanced through the creation of international organizations such as the ICC.

Adherents of this view believe that national leaders are capable of giving up some sovereignty to the ICC. . . . They are willing to surrender some national sovereignty because they believe that the rule of law can modify, or at the very least restrain, unwarranted and unwanted human behavior in the relations between nations and between groups within a nation.

These supporters of the independent ICC, nations such as Canada, Italy, Costa Rica, Sweden, and Norway, believe that the awesome terrors of genocide, crimes against humanity, and egregious war crimes are crimes of universal jurisdiction. They have had an effect on human societies, and the time has come for such an ICC. In their view, shared by the author, there is a civilized universal conscience. . . . When touched by injustice, human beings support international acts against the perpetrators of atrocities that defy comprehension.

Balancing Politics and Justice

Some observers sadly note that realpolitik "most likely will prevent the ICC from being a truly effective organ of justice." A noted liberal advocate, Aryeh Neier, wrote that "the heart says civilized men and women with respect for the rule of law cannot permit these kinds of [war] crimes to happen again. The mind, sadly, sends a different kind of message."

At some point, however, and the 1998 Rome convention is such a watershed, the world community has to say, enough killing! Even if it means the possible surrender of some national sovereignty, the killing has to stop. Sooner rather than later, nation-states must accept the concept of national submission (with adequate protections) to international authority with respect to jurisdiction over war crimes, crimes against humanity, and genocide. . . .

They (perpetrators of genocide) must be punished lest other genocidal leaders think that they have impunity for their evil plans, orders, and acts. Clearly, the humanity of the issue must be addressed by the opponents of the ICC. There is, I believe, an international civilized conscience that categorically rejects the continuation of genocidal warfare and that demands that the international community take substantive steps—quickly, without debates and filibusters in the Security Council—to end the horrible consequences of such crimes.

The world community must deny the perpetrators of genocide, war crimes, and crimes against humanity safe haven and impunity from punishment. The peoples of the world are ahead of their political leaders on this matter. Without the interference of realpolitik, they understand that those men and women who commit grave, grievous crimes against others, especially women, children, and the elderly, must be punished.

There must be a balancing of the two contending concepts—realpolitik and the need to provide justice for the victims of genocide and a complete trial record for posterity. If there is no resolution of the dynamic tension between them, the world community will enter the twenty-first century without a legal mechanism to punish such criminals. If that is the case, one must note the lack of moral commitment to the concepts of equity and justice for men and women.

As an idealist without illusions, I believe that the United States will sooner rather than forty years later support the ICC, either individually or through its participation in NATO. There are enough checks in place in the Rome statute to convince reasonable Americans that a runaway special prosecutor would be controlled or removed by the ICC Chambers. With a growing trust in the integrity of the ICC, especially its independent prosecutor, there will come a greater willingness to accept the organizational and jurisdictional structure and work to change it, if necessary, once the statute is ratified. If the powerful nation-states do not support the ICC, there will be no data on whether it is a successful deterrent to crime. Risky though it may be for America's public policymakers and military leaders to overcome their fears about the loss of sovereignty, it is a risk that must be taken.

President Bill Clinton was publicly chastised at the Washington, D.C., ceremony opening the United States Holocaust Museum on April 22, 1993, by the dedication speaker, Nazi Holocaust survivor and author Elie Wiesel, for not acting against the genocide taking place in Bosnia-Herzegovina. Turning to the president, Wiesel, who had recently returned from a visit to a Serb prison camp, said:

> Mr. President, I cannot not tell you something. I have been in the former Yugoslavia last fall. I cannot sleep since for what I have seen. As a Jew I am saying that we must do something to stop the bloodshed in that country. People fight each other and children die. Why? Something, anything must be done!

There was thunderous silence: Clinton did not respond to Wiesel. However, there must be more than silence in the face of war crimes, torture, crimes against humanity, and genocide. The world cannot tolerate these heinous crimes going unpunished, with the butchers of innocents given impunity by the silence of the powerful nations. The international community must move beyond silence to action.

THE USE OF U.S. MILITARY INTERVENTION TO PREVENT GENOCIDE

Michael O'Hanlon

In 1999 the United States and its European allies launched a two-month bombing campaign against Serbia in order to stop the Serbs' massacre of ethnic Albanians in the province of Kosovo. In the following essay, Michael O'Hanlon, a foreign policy scholar at the Brookings Institution, considers whether the Kosovo campaign could serve as a model for U.S. military intervention in other potentially genocidal situations. In some cases, O'Hanlon concedes, American military intervention might spark additional conflict that would result in a greater loss of lives, and thus should be rejected as an option. However, he contends, in other cases, outside military intervention could save hundreds of thousands of lives. The type of military intervention would depend on the particular circumstances of the situation, he writes, and might involve establishing secure havens for threatened populations.

Was the NATO (North Atlantic Treaty Organization) 1999 air campaign against Serbia just a onetime thing, or can the United States and other like-minded countries really stop genocidal wars around the world? Although this war is ending, we might face the question again soon. In recent years, the world has witnessed the 1994 Rwandan genocide, the 1992–1995 Bosnian civil war, and the 1992–1993 war-induced famine in Somalia. Even today, wars that have taken many more lives than the conflict over Kosovo remain unresolved in places such as Angola and Sudan.

We certainly cannot settle every conflict in the world. But the international community can generally do something about the worst wars—if not in every case, then at least in most. The question is how to decide when and where to intervene. Under the 1948 U.N. convention against genocide, the United States is, in theory, obligated to take major steps—up to and including the use of force—to stop genocide. In practice, however, the convention is not such a clear guide. It defines genocide as an effort to destroy, "in whole or in part," a national, ethnic, racial, or religious group. But does that mean that a

Reprinted from Michael O'Hanlon, "Saving Lives with Force," *The New Republic*, July 12, 1999. Copyright © 1999 The New Republic, Inc. Reprinted with permission from *The New Republic*.

dozen ethnically motivated murders qualify? Presumably not; other-wise, there would be genocides going on all over the world all the time.

Yes, some cases are clear, such as the 1994 genocide by Hutus against Tutsis in Rwanda. But was Serbia's war against the Kosovar Albanians genocide? In 1998 and early 1999, about 2,000 Kosovar Albanians were killed by Slobodan Milosevic's forces—a very modest number of combat-related deaths in comparison with many other wars around the world. However, Serbia's ethnic cleansing operations eventually drove hundreds of thousands of Kosovar Albanians from their homes, exposing them to deadly hunger and disease, and NATO now estimates that Serbian forces killed at least 10,000 mostly unarmed civilian Kosovar Albanians once the air strikes began.

Criteria for Intervention

Partly because of these ambiguities, former Representative Stephen Solarz and I have proposed that military intervention should be con-sidered whenever the rate of killing in a country or region greatly exceeds the U.S. murder rate, whether the killing is genocidal in nature or not. Our moral premises are twofold: first, since all human lives have equal value, the United States and other countries should use their military and political resources where they can save the greatest number of individuals. Second, the United States cannot be politically or morally expected to try to make other countries safer than its own domestic society.

The annual U.S. murder rate is roughly 1,000 people per every 10 million. According to our proposal, the United States and other coun-tries should strongly consider intervention where the intensity of killing or war-related starvation is several times greater—say five to ten times that number. To be sure, precise data about death rates in wars is rarely available. Nor should the world wait a whole year to determine an annual rate. And there will sometimes be cases where fewer deaths justify humanitarian intervention. For example, in Haiti in 1994 and in Kosovo in 1999, the fact that countries suffering civil violence were near to the United States and Western Europe provided an added rationale for action.

Generally, though, the criteria for intervention that Solarz and I have devised narrow the list of candidates for intervention. While wars in Algeria, Sri Lanka, Afghanistan, Iraq, the Congo, the Ethiopian-Eritrean border area, and a few other places have been severe, they haven't been nearly as lethal as others. As Solarz and I have argued, there were about eight extremely lethal conflicts between 1992 and 1997 that met our criteria: Sudan, Somalia, Rwanda, Burundi, Liberia, and Angola, as well as Bosnia and Chechnya. Since we first wrote on the topic in the Autumn 1997 *Washington Quarterly*, North Korea (where the famine stems from the government's tyranny and corruption and is therefore akin to a war) and Kosovo might have joined the list, making for a total of ten during the Clinton presidency. All told, these ten cases have accounted for more than 75 percent of all war-related deaths in the world since 1992.

How Should We Intervene?

Once we have reasonable criteria for determining which conflicts are so lethal that they may warrant intervention, the next question is: How do we actually intervene? First and foremost, since saving lives is an inherently political mission that will often be opposed by at least one local party to a conflict, intervening forces need to be braced to take sides; well-intentioned proposals for "separating combatants" and "disarming militias" may not work smoothly. Taking a side means that any intervention will require battle-ready combat units deployed in sufficient numbers to protect indigenous populations and themselves.

In a small, militarily weak country like Rwanda, it might have sufficed to send 10,000 to 15,000 troops. But, in gigantic Angola, where fighting is spread throughout much of the country, or in Kosovo, where the enemy has many tens of thousands of troops under arms and a good deal of heavy military equipment, an intervening force could easily require tens of thousands of troops.

With interventions of this magnitude, the difficulty then becomes getting troops into place quickly enough to stop the killing. In discussions about a possible ground war in Kosovo—and the logistical complications of deploying 100,000 or more fairly heavily armed forces to a remote part of the world with challenging terrain and underdeveloped infrastructure—some people suggested that any NATO ground invasion would have taken three or more months to prepare. While I believe that half that time would have sufficed—an intervention that emphasized Army air assault and Marine Corps forces could have been under way in a little more than a month—Kosovo is probably one of the most difficult interventions we would face. Yes, in most instances we'd likely encounter physical conditions just as challenging as those we would have faced in the Balkans, but the presumed enemy would not be as strong as Serbia.

In such situations, airborne and other light infantry forces, backed up by modest amounts of heavy weaponry, would generally be able to get the job done. And those units could be transported fast—10,000 to 20,000 troops can be moved virtually anywhere in the world within a couple of weeks, even to inland locations like Rwanda. The American C-17 transport aircraft can use most short runways; it and other large planes can also fly to a regional staging base and then transfer equipment to smaller C-130 aircraft and helicopters for a final approach.

And what about air power? Alas, NATO's partial success in Kosovo hardly proves that air power alone can stop civil wars. Most involve few heavy weapons that can be spotted and attacked from long range.

And, in less developed countries, there are few large strategic economic targets; bombing them as we bombed Serbia's infrastructure may exacerbate a humanitarian crisis without gaining great leverage over the factions that generally wage such wars.

The truth is that we cannot usually expect humanitarian interventions to be as casualty-free (for our forces) as the recent war against Serbia. Ground-combat missions are inherently dangerous. Dozens of Americans were killed in action in such relatively minor operations as Grenada, Panama, and Somalia. A lucky shot by a man-portable surface-to-air missile or even a rocket-propelled grenade could bring down an airplane or helicopter; that's how the Mogadishu debacle began for U.S. forces in 1993. Even poorly armed militias can successfully ambush Western forces in urban or forest settings.

Three Options

If we do intervene, we will generally have three kinds of options: (1) take sides, either overthrowing a reigning regime or helping one side in a civil war defeat the other; (2) impose and then enforce a partition line between two main geographic zones (not simply between different militias within a given city or region); or (3) set up safe havens or humanitarian relief zones to protect a threatened population from murder and starvation.

Even if the United States and like-minded countries choose the right time and place to intervene, they could easily go about it the wrong way. For example, waffling between a limited intervention to provide food relief in Somalia and aggressively seeking to eliminate one particular militia from the country's political scene cost eighteen American lives in October 1993. In Bosnia, setting up safe havens failed to make towns like Srebrenica anything close to safe. Using air power against Serbia in 1999 has produced an ambiguous result: ethnic cleansing may be largely reversed and Milosevic's aggression ultimately defeated—but at the cost of thousands of Kosovar Albanian lives and the wholesale destruction of their homeland. The wrong intervention may well be worse, or little better, than no intervention at all—not just for our own country but even for those we are trying to help.

Moreover, there will be times—even in cases like the ones that meet Solarz's and my criteria for lethality—when using force to stop genocide or other mass killing won't be appropriate. For a humanitarian intervention to be wise and ethical, it must be attempted only if the odds are excellent that it will make a bad situation better and not worse. Intervening to stop Russia from killing tens of thousands of innocent Chechens, for instance, would have risked a major-power war between nuclear-weapons states with the potential to kill far more people than the intervention could have saved. Invading North Korea to bring food to its starving people would probably precipitate all-out war on the peninsula, quite possibly killing as many civilians in Seoul (to say nothing of soldiers on both sides of the war) as the food aid would save in North Korea. Entering into the Angolan civil war would force us to choose sides between our former anti-Communist associate Jonas Savimbi, a maniacal killer who has already violated two major peace accords, and the corrupt dos Santos government.

In Rwanda, however, the sheer scale of the killing—nearly one million dead in several months' time in 1994—meant that almost any intervention would have been better than standing aside. The international community should have quickly sent at least 10,000 forces to defeat the genocidal Hutu militias that targeted Tutsis and moderate Hutus. Whether those forces then stayed on for years to help the country rebuild or took the radical step of partitioning Rwanda would in this urgent case have been a secondary concern.

In Sudan, we should also have intervened in the early '90s. In fact, the case for doing so may become compelling again, as the 1999 cease-fire shows signs of fraying. The most natural solution to end the fighting and associated famine would be to partition the country into two parts: a predominantly Muslim north and a predominantly Christian south. That would not please Western liberals who insist on promoting multiethnic democracies all over the world, but it could save hundreds of thousands of lives quickly, and at a modest blood cost to the United States.

In Liberia, the number of victims in the civil war during the first half of the '90s was much smaller than in Rwanda or Sudan. Nonetheless, the world should have intervened to stop the killing and help establish a coalition government and a professional military. Ethnic hatreds were less severe, and the violence more arbitrary and wanton, than in many other wars. Under those conditions, chances were good that the bloodshed could have been quickly stopped. Liberia's modest geographic size is an additional factor that would have lent viability to a possible intervention.

Giving Americans a Sense of Purpose

Does the United States really have to do the lion's share of the work in these types of interventions? Unfortunately, no other country is capable of doing so yet. But our European allies, and several other countries such as Canada and even Japan, should get better at deploying modest numbers of troops to distant combat zones. Granted, this improvement will take several years, even if the European Union's recent efforts to organize itself more effectively for power projection bear fruit. (Only Great Britain and, to a lesser extent, France are making any serious efforts in this direction at present.) As for the neighbors of a country where genocide or highly deadly warfare might be occurring, most would not be militarily capable of conducting operations beyond their own borders. Moreover, it's doubtful that neighboring countries—which may be predisposed to favoring a certain faction over another—are removed enough to play the role of a fair-minded outsider.

Stopping the world's worst wars is not always practical or worth the cost—sometimes our efforts will only produce a temporary peace. But we should have intervened in Rwanda, Sudan, and probably Liberia. In addition, we were right to get involved in Somalia, Bosnia, and Kosovo. At least in Somalia and Bosnia, hundreds of thousands of lives were ultimately saved—even if hundreds of thousands had already been lost by the time the interventions took place. If we had intervened properly in all six of these cases, we could have prevented about half of the world's war-related deaths since 1992 and, depending on how you apply the term, two or three genocides. Doing so would have required us to spend a couple percent more on defense than we did this decade. It might have cost dozens or even hundreds of American lives. But we could have saved literally millions of souls in the process—and given a country still searching for its place in the post–cold war world a much clearer and nobler sense of purpose.

AN EARLY WARNING SYSTEM CAN PREVENT GENOCIDE

Israel W. Charny

In the following selection, Israel W. Charny describes his proposal for a World Genocide Early Warning System. By tracking the prevalence of certain national attitudes and activities, such as tolerance of violence and the dehumanization of potential victim groups, it may be possible to foresee impending genocides in time for other countries to take action to prevent them, Charny maintains. He proposes ten early warning indicators that can be used to monitor the likelihood of an outbreak of genocide in a particular society or nation. Charny is the executive director of the Institute on the Holocaust and Genocide in Jerusalem, as well as the author of numerous books on genocide and the Holocaust. He is also a professor of psychology at Hebrew University in Jerusalem.

In collaboration with Chanan Rappoport, [I have] proposed the development of a World Genocide Early Warning System. This is based on a comprehensive model that attempts to develop the processes of being turned toward destruction of other human life both on the level of the individual psychology and on the level of collective group process. Utilizing a series of basic psychological needs in the psychological economy both of the individual and of groups, I track the unfolding movement of people and larger collective groups toward their definitive choices of whether to engage in genocidal destruction as a way of organizing themselves in the face of universal existential dilemmas. The same basic psychological mechanisms were then translated on a societal level into what I called Genocide Early Warning Indicators, and these were incorporated into a societal Genocide Early Warning System that is intended to stand in its own right as a framework for assembling information and issuing warnings of the emergence of actual genocidal events in the world community.

The concept of a Genocide Early Warning System has been published in a variety of articles and chapters, and has earned strong positive reviews from human rights specialists, societal scientists, and

Excerpted from Israel W. Charny, "The Prospects for a Nongenocidal World," in *Collective Violence: Harmful Behavior in Groups and Governments,* edited by Craig Summers and Eric Markusen. Copyright © 1999 Rowman & Littlefield Publishers, Inc. Reprinted with permission from The University Press of America.

some national leaders. Willie Brandt, former chancellor of West Germany, wrote, "Your plan to develop concepts and proposals for disseminating the information on the genocide and human rights data bank sounds fascinating. I would like to assure you that I am ready to give my moral support." A former U.S. deputy assistant secretary of state for human rights, Roberta Cohen, said, "Your proposal to establish a Genocide Early Warning System is an excellent idea. Had such a system operated effectively in the past, countless lives might have been saved in many parts of the world." *Choice,* a library review magazine, hailed the proposed early warning system as "brilliant," and it was noted by the *New York Times Book Review* as a "noteworthy contribution to thinking about the condition of humanity on the earth." In two known cases, scholars have successfully applied the model *retroactively* to reconstruct the unfolding sequence of a genocide, specifically the Armenian genocide and the Rwandan genocide. . . .

Collecting Information

The Genocide Early Warning System is to collect information on three levels. First and foremost, it is to assemble information of ongoing genocides and massacres in the world on a regular, authoritative basis. Second, it is to maintain a continuous monitoring of information of violations of human rights. Third, it is to be the basis for a series of researches to understand more of the patterns through which massacre, mass murder, and genocide build up in a society, so that we will learn how to predict and alert people to the increasing dangers of mass murders in different societies well ahead of time.

The purpose of the creation of a Genocide Early Warning System is not only to develop a center that will receive, house, and make available on a continuous basis informations of ongoing massacres in the world, but also to create a center that is an international agency on behalf of human society as it speaks for the intention of humankind to care about and protect human life. The informations to be delivered to society by the early warning system are not only to maintain updated factual information, but also to convey the presence of an international agency that represents the evolution of a humane society that intends to keep a spotlight on the wrongdoings of mass murder. The real purpose of early warnings of genocide is to help the world develop new energies and new forms for attacking mass murder long before the murderers have completed their horrible task (which is essentially what the millions of words written about genocides to date represent, namely, crying after the task is over).

The Genocide Early Warning System we planned is built on a conceptual structure that assembles information over a long term about the basic processes in each society that *support human life* and those that are moving toward the *destruction of human life.* Both processes are known to be present in all societies. A balance of these processes in favor of the protection of human life is the desired hallmark of a society that will be unavailable to engage in mass murder. Clearly, there are societies where, long before the mass murder is executed, the balance is very much tipped toward destruction of human life.

The Genocide Early Warning System identifies *ongoing processes* as differentiated from *critical incidents,* which are also recorded; the first refer to less dramatic but steady patternings of processes in a society such as the degree of protection of free speech, or the degree of discrimination of minorities, while the second refers to dramatic events such as a major turn in policy as a result of the emergence of a new leader, the impact of going to war, economic breakdown, and so on.

Another level of analysis assembles information about *societal processes* as a whole such as previously described in the way of a free press, or the role of law, along with the roles of *leadership* or the decisive decisions and implementations by heads of states or cultures such as presidents, prime ministers, dictators, church leaders, and so on.

These levels of information are studied along a time continuum that begins with the ongoing situation in a culture long before there may have developed what we call *the genocidal fantasy or ideology* in that culture. The monitoring continues by tracking when an idea of genocide begins to be widely proposed and approved in a society, and when it gains political support of groups of people who actually try to organize to implement the genocidal plan.

Early Warning Indicators

The early warning indicators formulated by myself and Rappoport . . . will be briefly explained here:

Early Warning Process 01. The Valuing of Human Life

The valuing of human life refers to the basic norms in any given society with respect to the degree to that human life is valued or not. The respect and value which are placed on human life are two of the important aspects of a culture when the time comes that the society is faced with a possibility of being drawn into committing mass murder of a target people.

Early Warning Process 02. Concern with the Quality of Human Experience

The concern that a society shows for the quality of human experience, and whether and to what extent the norms of society are that people should be given the opportunity to live out their lives as comfortably as possible with respect to basic shelter, food, medical treatment, opportunity to work, freedom from oppression, freedom of speech, and so forth.

Early Warning Process 03. The Valuing of Power

This early warning indicator refers to the ways in which power is valued in a society, and when the goals of power are to gain control over other people, dominate them, enslave them, and exploit them.

Early Warning Process 04. Machinery for Managing Escalations of Threat

This early warning process refers to the development of machinery for managing escalations of threat. There are dangers of subjective exaggerations and distortions in human experiences of threats so that there is a need for cross-checking of information and checks and balances on the powers of decision makers who formulate the policies of responding to dangers.

Early Warning Process 05. Orientation Toward Force for Self-Defense and in Solution of Conflicts

This early warning process refers to a society's orientation toward force for self-defense in its solution of conflicts, and the question of how much force should be used in response to varying degrees of threat aimed toward one's people. It is human to want to destroy our enemies completely, but not only are there dangers of misjudging threats (EWP 04), the use of force in self-defense in itself may be excessively brutal and destructive and no longer for defense as it is for brutality, sadism, and murder.

Early Warning Process 06. Overt Violence and Destructiveness

This early warning process involves a society's use of overt violence and destructiveness, and whether there are societal policies and safeguards to ensure that the police, army, and population at large not be unnecessarily violent. The degree to which violence is heralded, rehearsed, and taught on American television is obviously connected to the very real dangers too many Americans face from assault and murder in many cities across the great continent. A society that limits exposure to violence in its media, and develops more mature attitudes in its journalistic reports of actual events of violence, can also be expected to be less susceptible to being drawn into genocidal violence toward others.

Early Warning Process 07. Dehumanization of a Potential Victim Target Group

This early warning process refers to dehumanization of a potential victim target group or the assignment of targeted groups of peoples a status as *less-than-human* or *nonhuman,* therefore not deserving of the protections that human society gives to its bona fide members. When there does develop an actual momentum of a society to attack a given minority group, the extent to which that minority previously has been assigned a role of subhuman or nonhuman will play an important role even in the readiness of the soldiers on the front line to execute a policy of extermination.

Early Warning Process 08. Perception of Potential Victim Group as Dangerous

This early warning process is the perception of the potential victim group as dangerous. Strangely, the very people who are dehumanized often are also invested with superpowers and are attributed enormous physical, economic, religious, racial, or what have you powers to destroy one's own people, hence this becomes a justification for invoking self-defense mechanisms and efforts to seek to destroy them before they destroy us. The fact that these people also have been defined as not human then allows one to be cruel and brutal to them. Genocide is now fully possible.

Early Warning Process 09. Availability of Victim Group

The early warning system continues with a dimension of the availability of the victim group. *Responsibility for the victimization is always entirely that of the perpetrator, who must be condemned,* but without reducing respect for the victims or empathy of their plight, it also has to be noted that groups and nations who are to begin with too defenseless, weak, naive, and susceptible to being bullied and terrorized make the victimization process more possible.

Early Warning Process 10. Legitimating of Victimization by Leadership Individuals and Institutions

This indicator refers to an advanced stage in the development of genocide when a society's leadership actually endorses and ratifies the mass destruction. Genocide is legitimated by the leaders; the courts redefine the target group as not subject to legal protection; the churches bless the killings; and genocide becomes the way of the land and its people.

Action and Hope

The concept of an early warning system has been the subject of a series of commission studies by International Alert, headquartered in London. The organization was created to seek to implement real, relevant interventions in the face of emerging genocidal situations in the world. . . . The first secretary-general of International Alert in London was Martin Ennals, who had been secretary-general of Amnesty International for many years, but who came to believe that the time has come to move on to deal not only with government imprisonment and torture of individuals (which is what Amnesty specializes in, although it is also concerned with some broader aspects of extrajudicial executions by governments), but also with governments committing mass murder and genocide. International Alert seeks to intervene at the level of government and the international system as early as possible when news of mass murders arise.

A 1992 book, *Early Warning and Conflict Resolution*, by the secretary-general of Alert, Kumar Rupesinghe, together with Michiko Kuroda from the United Nations in New York, presents a contemporary overview of early warning work to date in the international system, which adds up, unfortunately, to just a bare beginning of empirical work, and yet also conveys the growing number of scholars and agencies who seem to be knowledgeable, interested, and perhaps on the verge of the first breakthroughs of implementation. . . .

There can be hope. Flying in the face of profound moral outrage and continuing despair over the continuation of despicable mass slaughters of human beings around the world, there can be hope, because the idea of delegitimating mass murder has appeared on the agenda of human evolution, and is earning the inspired attention and thoughtful creativity of scholars in a wide range of countries around the world.

REMEMBERING THE HOLOCAUST CAN PREVENT FUTURE GENOCIDES

David Matas

David Matas is a lawyer in Winnipeg, Manitoba, Canada, specializing in refugee law. He is the coauthor of *Justice Delayed: Nazi War Criminals in Canada*. In the following piece, Matas maintains that keeping the memory of the Holocaust alive is vital to the prevention of future atrocities. He advocates extensive education in the schools so that the generations who are too young to have personal memories of the Holocaust can gain an understanding of how and why it happened. Governments should also keep in mind the policies that allowed the United States, Canada, and other nations to turn a blind eye to early reports of the Holocaust and refuse to take in Jewish refugees who were attempting to escape the genocide. By remembering and assessing the events that led to the Holocaust, the world's nations may be able to prevent similar tragedies in the future, Matas concludes.

Why should the world remember the Holocaust, the Nazi-perpetrated genocide of the Jews? This is a question that seems almost ridiculous to pose. One would think that it goes without saying that the past—and genocide in particular—should be remembered. Nonetheless, what one person takes from granted, another does not. This essay examines the reasons for remembering the Holocaust.

Holocaust Deniers

An imperative reason for remembering is the contemporary rise of neo-Nazism. Although it is not an especially popular phenomenon, it indicates that the anti-Semitism that prompted the mass murders still exists. Moreover, it now often takes the form of denying that the Holocaust ever happened. Our remembering the past—affirming that it did indeed happen—relieves the victims of the burden of establishing the historical record.

Hate propaganda is becoming bolder and more pervasive, and indifference to it and to its consequences in the past only sows the seeds of future hatred. The activities of groups in the United States like the

Aryan Nations and the Liberty Lobby and of people in Canada like Jim Keegstra, Ernst Zundel, John Ross Taylor, Donald Clarke Andrews, Robert Wayne Smith, and Malcolm Ross are the harvest of past indifference. When governments ignore the Holocaust, it becomes that much easier for those who would deny that it happened and would perpetuate its evil.

The Need for Education

Although the crimes themselves were the work of a relatively few individuals, they were made possible by the passivity of whole populations. One task we must assume is to ensure that never again will a society in general remain passive in the face of mass murders organized by a few. To do this will require widespread education and a determined effort to remember history.

Education about the Holocaust belongs in the schools and in the history textbooks. Although extensive materials have been developed, many have been reluctant to use them. One program designed to overcome that reluctance has been that of the League for Human Rights of B'nai B'rith Canada, which offers to Canadian educators tours of the death camps of Europe, followed by a visit to Israel. The program, called "Holocaust and Hope," serves both an educational and a motivational purpose. Teachers return to their classrooms impelled by their experiences to pass on what they have seen and learned to their students.

The prosecution of Nazi war criminals can also serve an educational purpose. When the public learns of a particular crime committed during the course of the Holocaust, it makes concrete its overwhelming devastation. A trial, with daily media reporting, provides fresh insights into the Holocaust—its premises and its techniques. Nazi war crimes trials, of course, should not be conducted merely for publicity, but, rather, to bring mass murderers to justice. Once a trial is taking place, however, its educational value should not be overlooked. For instance, in Canada, during some trials, schoolchildren have been brought in to watch part of the proceedings.

Yet another reason for remembering the Holocaust is that soon all the perpetrators, all the surviving victims, all the witnesses, will be dead. Their memories must be recorded before it is too late. It is now forty-six years since the end of World War II. Those who were young adults then are now in their late sixties. As many survivors as possible should be interviewed and encouraged to recall their experiences. That has been done in order to prosecute Nazi war criminals, but there is another reason.

The survivors of the Holocaust represent the collective memory of those who died. Only the survivors can tell us who lived, who died, who helped, who hindered. Each survivor is a fount of information to be tapped. There are, of course, many memoirs, films, interviews, and recordings of survivors, but there still remains a tremendous work of documentation to be done. Yad Vashem in Israel serves as a repository of memories of the Holocaust. But though one repository in Israel is useful, it is not sufficient. The Holocaust should be remembered everywhere, not just in Israel.

In Winnipeg, my own city, the government of the province of Manitoba has erected on the grounds of the legislature a monument in the form of a stone Star of David. The names of all those who died in the Holocaust and who have surviving relatives in Manitoba are carved in the stone. That is an example of how a community can participate in remembering the Holocaust.

Lessons of the Holocaust

For remembrance to be truly effective, however, it should not be isolated from the rest of human experience. The Holocaust was in some respects unique: in its scope, its aims, its techniques; but genocide, incitement to genocide, and attempts at genocide are regettably all too common. If we dwell on the unique components of the Holocaust, if we do not learn its lessons and apply them to contemporary events, we will be "forgetting" the Holocaust in another sense. We must remember not only what happened but why and how it happened— the prevalent anti-Semitism, the use of hate propaganda to spread and deepen that anti-Semitism, the refusal, in the name of realpolitik, of the world community to object to state-sponsored anti-Semitism in Germany in the thirties, the failure of the world's nations to admit refugees trying to flee the oncoming Holocaust and then the Holocaust itself.

The story of the postwar reluctance to bring to justice many of the Nazi war criminals cannot be divorced from the story of the refusal of governments to help the Jews during the war. They are not two stories; they are two chapters in a continuing story. The Allies refused to bomb the camps or the railroads leading to them; they failed to provide ships and havens for refugees from Nazi Europe, to declare free ports, and to censure the Vatican for its behavior in relation to the Holocaust. That dismal record means that the world must make atonement. It must acknowledge its guilt by omission, its failure to act, which made the Holocaust possible.

Guilt for the Holocaust is shared worldwide because of all the people the nations of the world could have saved and did not. Canada must share this guilt because of its restrictive anti-Semitic immigration policy in place at the time. Of all the countries in the Western world, Canada's record was the worst. Indeed, it was easier for a Nazi to come to Canada after the war than for a Jew to come during the war.

There have been counterparts to the Nazi Holocaust, for all its horrors. It was preceded by the Armenian genocide perpetrated in Turkey. It has been succeeded by the killing fields of Kampuchea, the mass killings in Uganda under Idi Amin and Obote, and the wholesale disappearances in Argentina. Lessons learned from the Holocaust could have helped us deter these mass murders, which continue to plague the world.

The Example of Indochina

Recent events in Indochina illustrate what happens both when we remember the Holocaust and act accordingly and when we do not. Many, for example, recalled the Holocaust in the case of the Vietnamese boat people in 1979. But in contrast, the lessons of the Holocaust have been forgotten or ignored in dealing with the Khmer Rouge of Cambodia.

The forced expulsion of ethnic Chinese from Vietnam (following the end of the Vietnam war in 1975 and the unification of Vietnam under North Vietnamese communist rule) was compared by many to the Nazi genocide of the Jews. Singapore government official S. Rajaratnam commented that the Vietnamese being cast adrift on the open seas was "a poor man's alternative to the gas chambers." And U.S. vice president Walter Mondale was reminded of the failure of world governments meeting in 1938 in Evian, France, to find protection for Jewish refugees. More important, however, were the concrete actions that followed. A U.N. conference in Geneva in December 1978 resulted in various countries pledging to admit 82,350 Indochinese refugees over one year. By June 1, 1979, these commitments had increased to 125,000, and by July, to 260,000. The United States had doubled the number it would admit, 14,000 a month, and Canada had tripled its commitment.

The citizens of Canada were well ahead of their government, however. At the time the Canadian government announced its willingness to take in Vietnamese boat people, it also set up a system of private sponsorship, whereby any corporation or group of five individuals could sponsor a refugee. Officials said that Canada would match, with government sponsorship, every refugee privately sponsored; the number was limited only by the willingness and ability of private persons to undertake sponsorship. But the response was far greater than the government had anticipated, and eventually it reneged on its commitment, saying it would match only 25,000 privately sponsored refugees, even if individuals sponsored more. After the Conservative government reduced its commitment, it was defeated in Parliament in December 1979. Its backtracking on matching became an election issue, with the opposition Liberals campaigning on a platform of full matching. When the Liberals won the subsequent election in early 1980, full matching was restored.

If the Vietnam story is heartening, the Cambodia story is not. There has been total inactivity in the face of the Khmer Rouge genocide. The West [as of 1989] recognizes as the legal government of Cambodia a coalition that includes the Khmer Rouge. Cambodia and Western governments have signed and ratified the U.N. Genocide Convention, which obligates signatory states to prosecute and punish perpetrators of the crime of genocide. The Convention also allows any signatory state to bring before the World Court in The Hague any other signatory state that fails in this obligation. The Cambodian government has prosecuted no one for the Khmer Rouge genocide, yet no Western government has invoked the U.N. Convention to bring Cambodia before the World Court.

Zbigniew Brzezinski, national security adviser under U.S. president Jimmy Carter, described American policy in Cambodia by saying, "I encouraged the Chinese to encourage [Khmer Rouge leader] Pol Pot." Richard Cohen, a *Washington Post* columnist, wrote, "In effect U.S. policy remained ever thus," and he likened the situation to the Allies' supporting Hitler after World War II if he had survived and continued to fight the Russians. Hurst Hannum made a similar comment. He wrote that the reasoning that has led to other Asian states supporting the Khmer Rouge would have permitted Hitler to remain in power after the war, had Nazi Germany not been so thoroughly defeated.

The United States has been slow to bring Nazi criminals in America to justice, one reason being the extensive recruitment and use of Nazis in the cold war. The U.S. Office of Special Investigation, devoted to identifying and tracking down Nazi war criminals, was not established until 1978. Canada has been even slower. Its war crimes legislation was not passed until 1987. Britain has yet to begin prosecutions.

The Link Between Memory and Action

If we ignore the Holocaust now, we compound the ignominy of the past, the failure of the world's nations to help the Jews. We make a black record even blacker. But we cannot hermetically seal off Nazi war crimes in the past. What we remember of them determines our future. Remembering the Holocaust and changing our behavior in light of its lessons deals with the past—and also makes a statement of what we are, what we want to become.

Remembering the Holocaust is a measure of atonement. But atonement requires more than simply remembering; it requires action. We must prosecute those Nazi murderers who remain free to this day. We must bring to justice the Khmer Rouge responsible for the killing fields of Kampuchea. Remembering and acting are inextricably linked.

When we remember the Holocaust, the effort is, above all, for humanity. What we remember says something about ourselves, about our willingness to accept responsibility. The message we give by forgetting is that mass murder is acceptable. Is that the message we want to leave with history?

The Effectiveness of Local Tribunals in Punishing Genocide in Rwanda

Elizabeth Neuffer

In 1994 the United Nations established a special international criminal tribunal to try and punish those who had participated in Rwandan genocide, in which hundreds of thousands of members of the Tutsi ethnic group were killed. However, Elizabeth Neuffer writes, this process has moved at a snail's pace due to the sheer number of suspects and victims involved. In response, Rwanda has proposed the creation of special village tribunals to hear cases and investigate accounts of genocide. Proponents believe that local tribunals will provide swift punishment for those guilty of genocidal atrocities, Neuffer explains, while others express concern that the members of the local tribunals are likely to be biased against the Tutsis and will not provide proper justice. Neuffer is a scholar affiliated with the Open Society Institute, an international philanthropic organization that sponsors research on social issues. She is writing a book on postwar justice in Rwanda and Bosnia.

Close to once a week for the last six years [since 1994], Claire Kayitare has come to the prosecutor's office in Rwanda's capital to plead for justice. Waiting in a shabby, poorly lit building along with dozens of other Rwandans on similar missions, she has kept one aim in mind: to push for a trial date for her husband, accused of taking part in Rwanda's brutal 1994 genocide and behind bars ever since.

But, on her most recent visit, Kayitare abandoned her quest. In fact, she threw over any hope at all of conventional justice. Instead, she implored prosecutors to transfer her husband's case to a proposed gacaca (pronounced "ga-CHA-cha") tribunal—a traditional system in which village representatives, not a government court, judge the accused. "As it stands now, it's not justice, it's revenge," said a tearful Kayitare, a handkerchief in her hand. "At least under gacaca the truth will come out."

The Promise of Gacaca

Gacaca—roughly translatable as "justice in the grass"—is the Rwandan government's latest effort to apportion blame for the brutal genocide that six years ago took close to one million Rwandan lives. Once a traditional Rwandan means for settling village quarrels—such as who stole whose cow—and reintegrating offenders into the community, gacaca has been revamped to deal with genocide-related theft, assault, and murder. Local views about the government's plan are mixed. But this much is clear: It can't be much worse than the status quo.

Rwanda's Tutsi-dominated government had hoped things wouldn't get this bad. For years the government tried, at least rhetorically, to render justice and foster reconciliation between the country's Tutsi and Hutu populations. It once thought its courts, along with the International Criminal Tribunal for Rwanda in Tanzania, could mete out individual responsibility for war crimes. But mass atrocities meant a massive number of perpetrators, and it quickly became clear that the biggest question facing Rwanda's courts was neither guilt nor innocence but mathematics. There are 125,000 genocide suspects behind bars and only a handful of lawyers and judges to try them, since many were slaughtered during the genocide. Even with an infusion of foreign aid and new staff, Rwanda's courts have tried just 2,500 cases since 1996. At that pace, it would take 150 years to try all the accused. "In normal justice, we begin with the people who died and make a dossier. That's one million murder cases," notes Fiacre Birasa, the Justice Ministry's point man on gacaca. "One million murders—who did these? It would take us more than one million years. Can we continue down this road? Logically, no."

That's where gacaca comes in, aiming to deliver justice that is participatory, rehabilitative, and, most of all, swift. As currently proposed, tribunals would be established at the Rwandan equivalent of town, county, state, and federal levels—up to 10,000 tribunals across this country of six million people. In each tribunal, elected judges (replacing the village elders of old) would assemble the community, hear testimony, and investigate crimes. There would be no prosecutors or defense attorneys to delay proceedings, and judges would reward confession—offering a blend of reduced jail time and community service to those who admitted their guilt.

The genocide's masterminds would still go before regular courts, as would those who carried out particularly heinous atrocities, but the gacaca tribunals would handle the hordes of small-time offenders. In fact, the government hopes to dispense with an astonishing 125,000 cases in the next three years. Birasa whipped out his calculator to prove the point. The country's gacaca courts could try as many as 200 cases per day, he estimated. He entered some figures, then exclaimed, "Gacaca could try up to 75,000 people in one year!"

The prospect of a speedy trial has Rwanda's prisoners clamoring to go before gacaca tribunals, even though the system is barely off the drawing board. Parliament only began putting it in place in February 2000, amending the constitution to allow gacaca tribunals to be supervised by the country's supreme court. The hope was that parliament would approve the gacaca law in April and trials might start in the summer of 2000. Some think that schedule may now be delayed, since Rwanda's Tutsi-led government has been rocked by a spate of resignations, which culminated in the recent resignation of its Hutu president, Pasteur Bizimungu. Then again, Tutsi Vice President Paul Kagame, the country's real power broker, who has temporarily taken over the presidency, may push forward a gacaca vote to show that Bizimungu's exit has not hampered the government's ability to get things done.

Proponents claim gacaca is well-suited to Rwanda. There are few secrets in this tiny country the size of Maryland, where people live in small, close-knit villages and where even the genocide was carried out in broad daylight. Gacaca tribunals, advocates argue, will use the moral force of the assembled village to shame perpetrators into admitting the truth. And, once that has occurred, an appropriate, rehabilitative penalty can be quickly devised. "In Western law, only the accused, the judge, and the victims are involved—so you only get a small part of truth," said Justice Minister Jean de Dieu Mucyo. "But, if you involve many people in a trial together, you get the truth. Nothing stands between survivors and the implicated."

Criticisms and Concerns

But not everyone is so optimistic. About an hour outside Kigali, in a ridgeline village known as Taba commune, a group of female genocide survivors gathered in a mud hut in March 2000 to discuss the role gacaca will play in their lives. All were witnesses when the International Criminal Tribunal brought proceedings against their mayor, Jean-Paul Akayesu [who was convicted of genocide and sentenced to life imprisonment in 1998]. Their testimony has cost them dearly, although they say they don't regret it. Several have been harassed and threatened, and, when speaking to a stranger, they still insist on using their court-assigned pseudonyms. The problem with gacaca, several noted, is that in most communities survivors are too outnumbered to have a voice. Precisely because a gacaca tribunal draws on the moral force of the village, it is more likely to represent the views of the Hutu, who are the majority, than the Tutsi, who were the bulk of those killed. "The truth will never be known," scoffed Witness P.P. "You are one survivor, and, in front of you, you have twenty people and the family of that killer. What you say will not be considered. There will be no one else to confirm it." Victims' groups agree, fearing that gacaca will result in a blanket amnesty for genocidal killers.

Human rights advocates worry about gacaca for a different reason: They point to the utter lack of safeguards for defendants and fear the proceedings might devolve into a Rwandan version of the Salem witch trials. Gacaca is supposed to represent a kind of indigenous Rwandan justice. But the reality is that Rwandans don't have a long history of due process; they're used to submitting to authority. Many fear gacaca trials will end up not as popular justice but as another form of state control. Even government officials admit the risk. "Gacaca will have problems—it would not be honest to say it will be perfect," said Gerald Gahima, Rwanda's attorney general. "You are requiring people to sit in judgment of their friends, their relatives. The conflict of interest is apparent."

But, with tens of thousands of cases still pending, officials insist there's no other choice. "Ordinary courts can never deal with the backlog of all the cases. I think gacaca ought to be given a chance. If it doesn't work. . . ." Gahima's voice trails off, and he wipes his eyes tiredly. "Then we will simply have to try something else."

CHAPTER 4

ENDANGERED PEOPLES OF THE WORLD

THE STRUGGLE OF INDIGENOUS PEOPLE AGAINST EXTINCTION

Art Davidson

Art Davidson is a longtime activist for Native Alaskans and the author of several books, including Endangered Peoples, *from which the following is excerpted. Davidson argues that many of the world's indigenous peoples—the first people native to their lands—are facing cultural and even physical extinction through displacement by newcomers, misguided government policies, and harmful activities by multinational corporations. Indigenous people want not only the right to survive, he explains, but also the autonomy to determine their own future and identity. Davidson concludes that humanity must work together to respect and preserve cultural diversity.*

Today, it is not distance but culture that separates the peoples of the world. How to cross such chasms between peoples may be the central question of our time.

"I am a dark-skinned, white-haired Indian grandmother, and sometimes I begin to feel that I am invisible," says Patricia Locke, a Lakota Indian and my close friend for nearly thirty years. "People see through me at airports, on the street, and at the meat market. When I mention this eerie feeling to Indian friends, they tell me it happens to them, too. I'm afraid to ask Indian children about it. I know this invisibility must hurt them. What is it that so clouds people's vision that they cannot see us?"

This sense of being invisible, unseen, and misunderstood, so frustrating on a personal level, creates one of the cruelest ironies of our time. All around the world, enlightened people anxiously follow the fate of sea turtles, condors, spotted owls, black rhinos, and hundreds of other endangered species. But they forget—or never realize—that whole peoples can be endangered, too. Before our eyes, human diversity is vanishing, but few seem to notice. The battle lines of cultural survival cross every continent, but the skirmishes often take place out of the media's sight—hidden away in remote corners of a desert, a rain forest, an island, or a highland plain. In almost every country, indigenous peoples, the first people native to their lands, are fighting for their lives, their identities, and a future for their children.

There are still, by various counts, between two hundred and two hundred and fifty million indigenous people in the world. The threat to native peoples should not be mistaken for normal cultural evolution, which has always taken place. Over the course of human history, tribal people have emerged, migrated, joined with others, and faded away. But in our time as never before, distinct cultures are vanishing virtually overnight. Since the beginning of the twentieth century, more than ninety of Brazil's indigenous tribes have disappeared. The Chinese have forced countless Tibetans from their homeland and brutally suppressed those who remained. In Africa's Sudan, government troops have displaced three million tribal people. In Guatemala, in just the last fifteen years, forty-five thousand Indian women have become widows, two hundred thousand Indian children have been orphaned, and two million Indians have become refugees. In 1970, there were thirteen thousand Penan tribespeople living in the forests of Sarawak [a state of Malaysia on the island of Borneo]; two decades later there were fewer than five hundred. . . .

This forced march into oblivion has many field marshals, all of them bolstered by our common indifference, misconceptions, misapprehensions, and distortions of the truth. By some people, native peoples are overly romanticized; by others, they are denigrated and seen as an obstacle to economic progress. But neither view is accurate. What indigenous peoples really share is a deep concern for the survival of their homes, their ways, their cultures . . . in a word, their individuality.

Encounters with American Indians

Like many Americans, I saw my first Indian galloping across a television screen: It was Tonto riding his pinto alongside the Lone Ranger's white stallion. My first inkling that Indians were real people came to me when I was about nine. We lived in eastern Colorado, and after a windstorm in late March, I went out on the prairie with my father to look for arrowheads. I remember the first one I found. It was half buried in the sand, and as I bent over to pick it up, I suddenly realized that Indians, *Indians,* had actually *lived* here—right here among the rocks and sagebrush where I stood. Turning that carefully chipped piece of flint in my hand, I wondered for the first time, Where are they? Where did they go?

When I was twenty-one, I moved to Alaska, where I gradually began working with Native Alaskans, particularly Yup'ik and Cup'ik Eskimos on the Bering Sea coast. In time, I was adopted by Joe Friday, a widely respected Cup'ik elder, and was taken into his extended Cup'ik family. Over the course of twenty-five years, I have witnessed and shared in many struggles—over land, over hunting and fishing rights, and over self-determination. . . .

In 1973, I worked closely with the Yup'ik chiefs—the Village Council Presidents, as they call themselves—to draft a statement on the state of their culture. The result was a small book titled *Does One Way of Life Have to Die So Another Can Live?* Since then, in my travels to many other parts of the world, I have found that native peoples everywhere are wrestling with this dilemma. Do their cultures have to die? Is it inevitable that the Indians of the Americas, the Aborigines, the Maoris, Igorots, Ainu, and hundreds of other distinct peoples will all be made to disappear?

Survival Is Not Enough

But survival alone is not enough, and not what native peoples call for. Of all the obstacles indigenous peoples continue to face, one of the most fundamental is also the hardest for non-native people to grasp—that not everyone wants to join the mainstream. In the developed countries, many of us have grown so accustomed to our highways and shopping centers, careers and retirement plans, that we assume everyone everywhere desires our way of life, our material wealth, and all the conveniences and consequences that go with them. Yet native peoples all over the world echo the plea I first heard voiced by the Yup'ik elders of the village of Nightmute: "Please try to fathom our great desire to survive in a way somewhat different than yours."

In May 1992, this basic desire was given form and substance by more than four hundred indigenous leaders from the far corners of the earth. In Kari-Oca, Brazil, at the first World Conference of Indigenous Peoples, these delegates declared their desire "to walk to the future in the footprints of our ancestors . . . to maintain our inherent rights to self-determination, to decide our own form of government, to use our own laws, to raise and educate our children, to preserve our cultural identity.". . .

As we begin to understand, *really understand,* the issues of indigenous peoples, we quickly confront the fact that the destinies of both native and nonnative peoples are linked. We all face challenge of survival. Among the greatest of these is the need for sustainable lifestyles that would enable us to live in balance with nature. It is a terrible irony that as our resource consumption reaches farther into rain forests and deserts, it destroys the only remaining cultures that know how to live in balance with the environment. Their cultural extinction would be a loss to us all.

To appreciate fully our global interdependence, we of the developed nations need to see the earth's native peoples for who they are, appreciating the problems they face and learning the value of their knowledge and wisdom. . . .

For every culture described here, dozens of others might have been included. For every voice, every person's story, thousands of others are just as poignant and urgent. No matter where we live, our lives intertwine with those of indigenous peoples. No matter what the color of our skin or what language we speak, we all have a personal stake in their future. Our response to the survival crisis of indigenous peoples will determine whether our era will be remembered as the time when much human diversity disappeared—or that when the earth's peoples finally learned to live together. . . .

What Can Be Done?

Several years ago, I thought that 1993, the Year of the World's Indigenous Peoples, might become a turning point in the struggle of these groups to survive. But for all the good intentions of the United Nations, its member states have made little more than token gestures toward the rights and needs of indigenous peoples. Far from assuring the cultural survival of these peoples, we are just beginning to understand the extent of the problem.

By some estimates, about two hundred thousand indigenous people a year are being killed. This is many more times the number of U.S. troops killed in Vietnam, casualties that sent a generation of Americans into shock. And the slaughter goes on year after year. Linguists now predict that fewer than half the world's six thousand languages will survive our children's generation. In the coming century, 90 percent of humankind's languages are likely to disappear. Perhaps the most astonishing thing about this unprecedented loss of humanity is that so few people seem to notice. In North America, for example, fifty-one languages have become extinct in just the last thirty years. But who can name even one of them? Who knows who these people were?

When are we going to draw that proverbial line in the sand and say, "Enough is enough"? It is true that we have no easy solutions, no tourniquet that can quickly stem this hemorrhaging of humanity. But, as indigenous leaders have been urging, certain important steps could make a real difference. The United Nations could adopt a strong Declaration of Indigenous Rights. Multinational corporations could routinely assess the effects of their activities on indigenous peoples. The developed countries of Europe, North America, and Asia could stop sending aid to countries that blatantly violate the human rights of native peoples. Churches could begin respecting indigenous beliefs, songs, and dances. The World Bank and other lending agencies could reconsider the progress-fixated worldview that has dictated their decisions and undermined so many indigenous cultures. And wherever we live we could demand that our governments protect native lands and ways of life, and the people's right to worship.

I'm afraid, however, that even the best laws, treaties, covenants, policies, and initiatives will be of limited value unless all people come to respect and value "the Other." Such an affirmation of humanity, *all* humanity, can only begin close to home—with the world's children, its schools, and its communities. Only from expressions of mutual respect on a small, local scale will it be possible to foster a broadened sense of responsibility.

In the global activities of nation-states and multinational corporations, lines of responsibility become obscure and hard to trace. Caught up with the busyness of our daily lives, we tend not to notice what is happening on the other side of the earth. It is not that we are callous or mean-spirited, but that living in a global community requires a kind of understanding that we have yet to develop.

But is "the Other," on the other side of the fence or the other side of the world, really such a mystery? Don't most of us work toward the same life goals—to provide food, shelter, and clothing for our families, to raise our children in peace, and to live in a clean and healthy environment? Native or nonnative, we all share hopes and dreams for a sense of safety and the opportunity to live life as we understand it. . . .

In the end, then, the answer to this daunting challenge to the world's cultural diversity is, in principle, dismayingly simple. We need to acknowledge that diversity is the great wellspring of humanity's strength, and then work as partners—all of us—to preserve it.

THE UNSETTLED FATE OF THE TRIBES
OF THE AMAZON

Diana Jean Schemo

The upper portion of the Amazon River in the tropical rain forest interior of Brazil is home to the largest concentration of isolated tribes of native peoples in the world, writes Diana Jean Schemo in the following article. Historically, she explains, these Amazonian Indians have fared poorly after coming into contact with white settlers, who often destroy their villages; many tribes have been driven to near-extinction. In an attempt to protect Brazil's remaining indigenous peoples, a few government officials promote a policy of limiting contact with newly discovered tribes and safeguarding their lands from encroachment by settlers. However, Schemo relates, many Brazilians oppose this policy because it restricts their access to the rain forest's resources. Schemo is a reporter for the *New York Times* and former chief of its bureau in Rio de Janeiro.

For Domingo Neves de Souza, it was only a half-hour's walk to the edge of the unknown. In September 1997, he ventured out from the Brazilian rubber plantation where he lived to go fishing. With his two daughters and three of their friends, he pushed deep into the western Amazon, following a winding tributary of the Igarapé River. Hidden in the thick surrounding forest, de Souza had long been told, were naked Indians who still set their lives to the forest's rhythms, just as they had for thousands of years: eating what the forest grew, hunting by bow and arrow. But for the 33-year-old rubber tapper, these Indians were an invisible presence, felt more than seen. Until that day, when they stepped out from the trees.

"Papa, there are people coming," yelled de Souza's 14-year-old daughter, Francisca. According to Francisca's later account, five Indians ran toward them, one dressed in shorts, the others naked. They carried bows and arrows, and were already reaching for them.

"Run, my girl, they'll kill you," de Souza cried as the arrows flew. One hit his left side. Another pierced his back. Turning around, Francisca saw

Reprinted from Diana Jean Schemo, "The Last Tribal Battle," *The New York Times Magazine*, October 31, 1999. Reprinted with permission from *The New York Times*.

the Indians closing in on her father. As she later reported, she knew right then she would never see him alive again.

An hour later, a posse of rubber tappers headed out to the spot. They found de Souza's body and saw that arrows were only part of the ordeal that had ended his life. Gashes covered his legs, chest, and head; all that remained of his eyes were the dark, bloody pools of their sockets. His scalp had been sliced from his skull. The Indians that Francisca and the other children described had vanished, as if soaked back into the forest. But who could they be? Were the killers really *indios bravos*—"wild Indians"—as the locals called isolated tribesmen? Or had the children's imaginations spun out of control? The rain forest grows rumors along with species, and stories multiplied.

These stories eventually reached the ears of Sydney Possuelo, the Brazilian government's leading authority on isolated Indians. Possuelo soon traveled to the area where the murder occurred, in the far western state of Acre—but not to solve the crime. For one thing, he was no police detective. What's more, Possuelo had little sympathy for ambushed pioneers; he knew that from Brazil's first days white settlers had ruthlessly slaughtered Indians, burning their villages and abducting their children to work as slaves. The reason he went to Acre was this: a murder by unclothed Indians has often been the first sign of a previously uncontacted Amazon tribe. If isolated people were indeed hiding nearby in the forest, Possuelo wanted to find them—but not to punish them. He wanted to offer the tribe protection, for as long as possible, from the modern world.

Isolated Indians and Their Protector

Anthropologists believe the Amazon shelters the world's largest number of still-isolated Indians. (The Pacific island of New Guinea is a distant second.) Since the 1970s, Brazil's government has counted fifty sites that reveal signs of indigenous settlement—many spotted by canvassing the rain forest from the air—though no known tribes are thought to inhabit those particular areas. Possuelo says that these traces were left by approximately fifteen tribes of the rain forest that have never been studied or, in some instances, even named by scholars.

By definition, little is known about isolated Indians. Their relics surface in the most remote stretches of the Amazon, hundreds of miles from the nearest roads. It is not known whether the tribes fled to these regions as Brazilians claimed more of the countryside or whether they were always there. Some tribes, like the Igarapé Umeré, in the state of Rondônia, have turned up like the straggling survivors of a shipwreck, with only a handful of members left. By contrast, the Korubu of the Javari Valley reach into the hundreds.

Standing between these tribes and the rest of the world is Possuelo, 59, who has pinpointed seven new tribes in his forty years as a *sertanista,* the peculiarly Brazilian occupation of Indian tracker. He can look at a footprint in the forest and tell instantly whether it belongs to a forest Indian or a Brazilian settler by the gap between the first two toes: Indians always walk barefoot, so the big and middle toes splay from repeatedly gripping the earth. Over the years, his own foot has come to resemble those of the Indians. But if Possuelo is the world's link to the mysterious tribes of the rain forest, he is also the most formidable obstacle to the rest of the planet's ever knowing them.

As director of the Indian protection agency's department of isolated Indians, Possuelo has almost single-handedly redefined his agency's traditional role. In the past, the agency, known as Funai, aggressively paved the way for white development of regions occupied by indigenous peoples. But Possuelo argues that virtually every tribe touched by Brazilian society has been destroyed as a result. Rather than flourishing from the medical and technological advances civilization could offer, they have withered from disease, slavery, alcohol consumption, and the greed of Brazilians. The numbers bear Possuelo out: the anthropologist Darcy Ribeiro's landmark book, *Indians and Civilization,* concluded that 100 Indian nations disappeared in Brazil between 1900 and 1970, the year his book was published. When Europeans first reached Brazil about 500 years ago, estimates of the Indian population ran from one to six million. It is now 300,000.

An irascible idealist, Possuelo clashes frequently with Brazil's entrenched economic and political interests. Sometimes, the *sertanista's* outrage at corruption within his own agency is so frank that it seems as if he parachuted into Brazil from another galaxy and will soon be blasted back. Possuelo's last boss tried to fire him in 1996, calling him insubordinate. But Possuelo's standing was so high—particularly among foreign environmentalists and Indian rights advocates—that his boss backed down. As President of Funai in the early 1990s, it was Possuelo who demarcated the largest Indian reservation in the world, 20.5 million square acres, for 23,000 Yanomami Indians, at least temporarily stemming an onslaught by gold miners against the world's largest surviving Stone Age tribe.

Possuelo argues that much as endangered turtles and jaguars deserve government protection, Brazil's Indians also need sanctuaries where they can rebuild their numbers and protect their cultures. Ranged against him is a chorus of powerful voices coming from those coveting Indian lands and resources, and their allies in the Brazilian government. "It won't do to have Indians in the 21st century," a former government minister, Helio Jaguaribe, has said. "The idea of freezing man in the first stage of his evolution is, in truth, cruel and hypocritical."

Others claim that Funai hypes the numbers of hidden tribes to prevent Brazilians from exploiting the country's wealth of natural resources. Critics also note that Brazil's Indians represent less than

0.25 percent of the population and yet claim 11 percent of the national territory. Then there are the missionaries, who covet the primitive soul. Don Pederson, who is in charge of research and planning for New Tribes Mission, a Florida-based group, argues that uncontacted tribes are plagued by malaria and dental problems, troubles for which the non-Indian world has ready solutions. "Would you say that you should leave people in dire straits in the ghetto because that's their area, and to go in and provide economic or health assistance is wrong because it would change their lifestyle?" asked Pederson, who has lived with the Yanomami and other tribes.

Still others are knocking on the Amazon's door. The state petroleum company, Petrobas, has made tentative explorations for oil in the Javari Valley. Pharmaceutical companies are hankering to patent genetic materials and forest-based cures. And linguists and other scholars want to track the languages of these unknown peoples.

But it's not only academics and industrialists who are interested in the tribes of the Amazon. At his apartment in Brasilia, Possuelo recently got a letter from a Swedish child, Karin Bark. The girl revealed that she had learned in school about the Korubu tribe, whom Possuelo first contacted in October 1996, and had grown curious about these newly discovered members of the human family.

"Do they eat insects?" she asked. "How many are they? How old can they become? Please answer my questions and tell me other things about the Korubu Indians.

"I want to know."

In Search of Lost Tribes

I, too, wanted to know. And so in July 1999 I joined Possuelo on a journey into the depths of western Brazil's rain forest. Once there, we would fly over the canopy in search of the tribe that may have violently announced its existence in Acre. Then Possuelo would lead us by boat into the jungle, where he would establish contact once again with the elusive Korubu.

Getting to the Amazon was complicated. We first found ourselves in the outpost town of Jordão, a listless place of high unemployment 120 miles by river from the Peruvian border. Jordão is so remote that it takes eight days by boat to reach the nearest Brazilian city, Rio Branco. The night we arrived, I visited the home of Octavio da Rocha Mello— the owner of the plantation where Domingo de Souza had worked. Like most of the houses near the riverbanks, Mello's tiny house was built on stilts. Inside, candles provided weak light.

Mello described de Souza's murder as part of a silent war by Indians to push whites out. After the killing, he claimed, naked Indians showed up at the local schoolhouse, terrifying the children. People stopped going to the river to bathe in the evening. The tappers, whose work involves trekking through the forest each day, began staying close to home. After twenty three years as the local master of the forest, Mello found his jungle fiefdom collapsing.

"It didn't used to be like this," Mello complained. "If the Indians killed a white person, there used to be people who would *go after them!*"

The next morning, I headed with Possuelo to Jordão's airport, a ribbon of dirt running through the center of town, to make our flight over the treetops. It seemed as if everybody in town had come out to watch us wait for the skies to clear. Possuelo sat on the wheel of a single-engine plane and listened as jobless locals complained about being driven out of the forest by *indios bravos*.

Luis Pinheiro de Lima, a 78-year-old Kaxinawa Indian reared by rubber tappers, spoke even more brutally than the whites. He said the government should go back to its old policy of dominating Indians, casualties be damned. De Lima called isolated Indians *bichos*, or "beasts," and recalled how tappers used to be able to send out mercenaries to hunt down Indians with dogs: But now, he said darkly, Funai "says you mustn't kill them."

Possuelo did not interrupt as de Lima mocked the forest Indians for eating only what they find in the forest, "everything roasted." But then he looked at de Lima and spoke in a voice that sounded almost sad. The practice of "civilizing" Indians killed a lot of your cousins, Possuelo told the old man. "There are still women with the names of the rubber plantations that enslaved them tattooed on their arms. *You know them.*"

Airplane Searches

In June 1998, from the same crumbling airstrip at Jordão, Possuelo hired a single-engine plane to fly him over the rain forest surrounding the rubber plantation in Acre. He was looking for a sign, however small, of human life.

As far as Possuelo could see from his plane, there was only forest, thick and impenetrable. Finally, after twenty hours scouring just this piece of the Amazon, he saw something. Barely visible through the forest canopy, he spied a clearing in the jungle, with long, narrow Indian huts covered with leaves. A few miles away, he saw another group of huts, similarly built, and a clearing for crops. As his plane flew over, he glimpsed unclothed Indians running into the forest.

With the power of Funai behind him, Possuelo quickly set about cordoning off the area, demarcating a 580-square-mile zone settlers could not legally enter. On a later trip, he found yet a third group of dwellings nearby, less than six feet tall, which suggested a tribe that did not sleep in hammocks. During the ensuing year, he told me, he heard through deputies that one tribe had built more houses and planted more crops. He wondered if relatives had migrated, creating yet more clearings in the canopy.

That's what he was looking for the day we flew together over the forests of Acre. With the sky half-clear, our small plane trundled in and out of the clouds like a growling, airborne dinosaur, passing over miles of uninterrupted treetops. Flying low because of the weather, we could survey only a small area at a time. Normally, Possuelo's work is painstaking, like combing the ocean floor for buried treasure. Indeed, to my eyes the rain forest seemed like an ocean of trees, stretching green as far as we could see in every direction. This time out, however, Possuelo knew where to look.

About fifteen minutes after taking off from Jordão, I glimpsed the sight that had so thrilled the *sertanista*. Through an opening that was little more than a keyhole in the forest canopy, I saw a group of long huts, with pitched brown rooftops like upturned canoes. They appeared to be about 50 feet long, 20 feet wide, and 10 feet tall—big enough for several families. We saw no crops planted nearby. The clouds were maddening, like a camera shutter allowing us only brief glimpses of the panorama below. Suddenly, my eyes were drawn to a young naked girl running out of a hut. I wondered if she was fleeing her home because of the sound of our plane. The girl did not look up or behind her, but disappeared quickly into the forest, as if it were a blanket she could pull over herself.

Though I burned to pass over again for another look, Possuelo would not hear of it. He does not even like to fly over hidden tribes once, suspecting that airplanes frighten the tribespeople and sometimes cause them to pack up and move. Indeed, Possuelo has never actually looked into the eyes of these Indians he risks his life to protect. He has never heard their voices or shaken their hands—and probably never will.

A Harsh Existence

Back in Jordão, José Carlos Mireilles, the grizzled chief of Funai for the state of Acre, told me that he sometimes questioned his boss's efforts to protect Indians. Isn't conquest a natural part of human history? Quite apart from the whites, aren't the tribes perennially raiding and killing one another?

Mireilles lived for eight years with Acre's recently assimilated Jaminawa tribe, believed to be closely related to the unnamed tribe Possuelo and I had just flown over. He is not blind to the harsh edges of Indian cultures. Jaminawa youth experiment with sex even before puberty, and girls who become pregnant before marriage undergo painful abortions performed by kneading the abdomen. Sometimes, Mireilles said, the abortion does not work, and the baby is born. In those cases, the unwanted babies are buried alive.

Thirteen years ago, the Jaminawa summoned Mireille's wife, a medic named Teresa, to deliver the baby of an unmarried teenager. She trekked through the rain, working until morning. But upon the baby's birth, the tribe lay the newborn in a small grave that had already been dug. Teresa Mireilles was horrified. "No way," she said. She took the boy from his grave, wiping the dirt from his nose. Mireilles and his wife consider the boy their son.

But if Mireilles does not hold a romantic vision of Stone Age life, neither does he bear illusions about the wonders Brazilian society has to offer. Throughout the twentieth century, even well-meaning whites have destroyed tribe after tribe, usually by introducing germs and diseases against which the Indians have no defenses: chickenpox, malaria, tuberculosis, the common cold. Other times, Funai has either connived, or unwittingly aided, in the systematic plunder of Indian lands and resources.

"If I could give them 10 or 20 years more without anybody bothering them, I think it's worth it," Mireilles said. "The day the Indians would come out of the forest, I'd tell them: 'Go back to the forest. There's nothing for you here.' "

Encountering the Korubu

From Jordão we flew north to Tabatinga, a ramshackle town located at the point where Peru, Colombia, and Brazil converge. There, we began our boat journey to visit the Korubu. For Possuelo, this was a homecoming of sorts. He had been away from the Amazon for nearly a year, following a near-fatal car crash that split open his skull, broke his legs, and knocked out an eye. Throughout the trip, as he ran into friends he hadn't seen, Possuelo doffed his cap and dropped his head, to show stitches running like expressways over his shiny crown, as if he still could not get over having survived.

After floating southwest for nine hours down the Javari River, we reached the sullen frontier town of Atalaia do Norte. Possuelo's boat pulled in to dock, but he did not stretch his legs on dry ground. Instead, he stayed on board the *Waika*, the boat that is his home for most of the year. With the area's thirteen sawmills silent these days, Possuelo had become the enemy—and he knew it.

The Indian lands upriver brim with timber and freshwater turtles and fish. It would all be there for the taking, were it not for Possuelo. When Funai first planted its flag at the Javari Valley reservation, roughly the size of Florida, it was the mayor of Atalaia himself who yanked it from the ground in protest. In the streets of the town, residents glared at us. Motor scooters came threateningly close, then made another pass so there was no mistaking their enmity. At the suggestion of the local police, the *Waika* pulled out in a hurry.

It was three years ago that Possuelo established the first peaceful contact with a fragment of Korubu Indians living in the Javari Valley. Having somehow separated from their tribe about 60 miles north, these Korubu were being ambushed and hunted down by local settlers. A fierce people, the Korubu were nicknamed the *caceteiros*, or "head bashers," for the way they killed enemies. They had already clashed with local Brazilians, once murdering two workers from the Petrobas oil company as hundreds of colleagues watched in astonishment. They had no history of peaceful contact.

On our trip, Possuelo had with him six Indians from tribes whose languages he guessed the Korubu might understand, headed by Bina, a Matis Indian whose face was tattooed to resemble a leopard's, with ten black lines running like whiskers over his cheeks. Bina's mother was Korubu, abducted as a child during a Matis massacre of the Korubu more than forty years before. Bina's own tribe had only made contact with Brazilian society when he was a boy.

Possuelo made four forays into the jungle in 1996, each lasting about ten days, before a small group of Korubu emerged from the leaves to meet him. They were naked and painted with rust-colored patterns on their faces and chests. Short and sturdy, the Korubu walked with their legs wide apart, as if to frighten off animals, and they appeared robust and confident, masters of their small universe. "How beautiful," Possuelo had whispered to himself.

We floated toward the Javari Valley frontier all day. Possuelo reveled in sudden problems, like a broken searchlight and engine trouble, that only his expertise could fix. There was a malaria epidemic sweeping the region, and Possuelo, who had already had malaria 36 times, was headed for bout 37—yet he was cheerful. Along the way, blue-and-silver dolphins turned cartwheels alongside the boat. Possuelo smiled. "Nature seems to want me back," he said.

The *Waika* chugged up to a government outpost, our final destination, an hour after midnight, nineteen hours after we began. With lights finally out and the motor silent, I caught the first movements of the local symphony. Bats fluttered overhead, locusts rattled like maracas, and owls sang a haunting chorus. From far away came calls I could not identify. Yet they sounded as if they were being repeated and perhaps answered, in the morse code of the jungle.

Could that be the Korubu?

At daybreak, sounds came from across the river. Emerging from our hammocks into the sunlight, we saw six Korubu, square shouldered and tan, with babies resting on mothers' hips. One man wore a polo shirt, but the rest were naked. "*Bina! Bina!*" a man's voice called over the water, steady and insistent. Our translator had returned to the government outpost since the initial contact and the Korubu remembered him.

The Korubu called to Bina: "We're hungry. Go hunting for us."

A group of Korubu, many of them suffering from malaria, had been camped across the river for days, far from their crops, and had had little to eat. Bina decided to help. He hopped into a speedboat docked next to the outpost and disappeared into the Indian areas with a hunting party. He returned a few hours later with wild boars and crocodiles, blood splattered on the seats.

With two of the animals lying on the speedboat floor, Possuelo crossed over to the Korubu, who swarmed to the boat and surrounded him in bursts of sound. Their voices were loud; to my ears, their language sounded bold, even harsh. I watched from a few feet away, in a separate speedboat. The Korubu men wore only a string that was fastened around their hips and looped around their penises; they stood with their chests out and shoulders thrown back. Two Korubu women slid down the riverbank, splashing water over their children to cool down. As the group took us in, they seemed almost angry. "*Pawa! Pawa!*" some declared. Suddenly, one member of our group unzipped a fanny pack and produced a soup spoon. The anger dissolved into wide smiles.

The following day, we returned to the outpost. There we found Xikxu, the patriarch, who looked about thirty-five. He called for the women, who emerged from the forest. One carried a child over one shoulder and a monkey over the other. "*Pawa, pawa,*" two of the Korubu women said, checking my pockets for spoons.

The women carried empty pots and bowls, showing them to me in a wordless version of a shopping list. This time, I understood: the Korubu live in a pre-metal age, and 8,000 years is long enough to wait for a damned spoon. Through Bina, I promised not to show up again empty-handed.

A young mother, baby perched on her hip and nursing, approached me slowly and touched my curly brown hair. Her own straight black hair was elaborately cut, shaved short in a band across the top of her head and trimmed one length across her temple and at the nape. Tugging the front of my shirt, she gestured for me to open it. She took out my breasts, showing the others that I was built like them. Then she looked down my pants, just to make sure. As direct as she was in her actions, the young mother, who appeared to be no more than eighteen, smiled gently.

"Maya Washeman," she said, pointing to herself. She pointed to another Korubu woman with a scar across her cheek. "Maya Mona," she said. She gestured at the sad-eyed woman sitting away from us, whose face I recognized from pictures taken of Possuelo's first contact back in 1996. "Maya Doni," she said. Then she pointed at me.

"Maya Diana," I told her.

I wasn't quite sure what "Maya" meant, but it seemed appropriate. But then I was introduced to Washeman's mother. Her name was Maya. Perhaps daughters identified themselves through their mothers' names. Bina couldn't say for certain.

With Bina's help, Washeman asked if I have children of my own. I said no. Then she handed me her own infant son to hold. This remarkable ambassador, I discovered, was the *casus belli* of her entire tribe.

Sitting on the ground, the Indians, through Bina, told a long story. They said they fled from their home tribe when Washeman reached puberty and a Korubu boy wanted to marry her. Maya, however, did not want the boy for her daughter and so fled with her clan. The boy ran after Washeman, kidnapping her. Undaunted, the family turned around and kidnapped her back. They said they ran for months, eventually carving a small canoe to cross the Ituí River. They ran until reaching Ladario, the closest white settlement, where they found bananas growing and stole some for the tribe. By way of introduction, they said, the townsfolk of Ladario chased the Indians and killed two of them.

Since then, the rest of the tribe had secretly been watching Ladario, and—incredible as it seemed, given the gulf in languages and the fear they must have had to overcome—they could identify the killers by name. "Otavio," Xikxu told Bina. Hearing the name chilled me; visiting Ladario the day before, I met the head of the settlement, Otavio Oliveira. He said he was a great friend to the Indians.

Cultural Dislocation

On the third day, Possuelo and I paid the Korubu one last visit, this time with some medicine for those suffering through malaria. It was cool under the trees, and quiet. Washeman touched the nape of her son's neck, putting my hand there so I could feel his fever. A few feet away, Maya, the matriarch of the clan, whimpered quietly. She, too, was burning up.

Xikxu scraped a rope-thick vine back and forth over a grater. A liquid the color of worn leaves trickled down. The grater was a wooden club like a miniature baseball bat, flattened on one side, with the chewing end of monkeys' teeth sticking out of the wood.

"Sometimes they drink hallucinogens before they kill somebody or go to war," Possuelo told me quietly in Portuguese, passing the drink. I took a sip, not knowing whether we were drinking the aperitif for war or death. It had the sour, very green taste of something unripe, something that had not found its natural flavor yet. After a few minutes, Possuelo quietly asked Bina about the juice. Bina revealed that the drink was just a social one. In the back of Possuelo's mind, and mine, was the story of the last station chief, Sobral, who angered the Korubu by taking back a tarpaulin one of Sobral's workers had given them. Two Korubu clubbed the government agent to death as his colleagues looked in horror from across the river.

Talking to Possuelo, the Korubu laughed over their first meeting with him and remembered hiding when his small plane flew overhead looking for them. Xikxu asked Possuelo why he smoked cigarettes, and Possuelo said it was something Brazilians do socially. As they listened, the Korubu said "mmm," in the same way Americans say "uh-huh." Seemingly apropos of nothing, Washeman asked Bina a startlingly frank question: "How do you have sex?" The question took us all aback.

"We do it at night," Bina responded.

Sitting there in the jungle, I began to wonder if the Korubu could truly fathom the difference between our world and theirs. And if history proved any guide, I thought, that knowledge, when it came, would shatter them.

In Darcy Ribeiro's book, the son of a *sertanista* describes the first exposure of Kaingáng Indians to São Paulo, which he witnessed as a child. The tribe had encountered Brazilians only two years earlier, when Funai began offering the Kaingáng gifts, like pots and machetes. The Indians saw the gifts as a tribute, and reckoned that they must be far more powerful than this small tribe of Brazilians visiting them in the forest. "Don't worry—we'll protect you," the Kaingáng chief told the government agents. But then one day the *sertanista* wanted officials in São Paulo to see the isolated Indians for themselves, so he took two of them to the big city.

"They entered the car and took their seats, and appeared talkative and happy as they crossed the forest," Ribeiro writes. "At the first station, as they watched the comings and goings of passengers boarding and disembarking, the Indians exchanged remarks. The stations went by, each one more full of people, because they were already crossing more densely populated regions. A sadness and a humiliation set in among the Indians; they stopped chatting and no longer even answered the Government agent's questions. Astonished, they got off in São Paulo." After being shuttled around the city, the chiefs returned to the jungle, disillusioned. They explained to their people how insignificant they were compared with the modern world. As Ribeiro notes, "Afterward, the prestige they attributed to the whites was of such an order that no tribal value could survive."

At the riverbank, the Korubu showed us a reed they call *nypuk*. The Indians peel the *nypuk's* sides until it looks like a blade of grass; its long, sharp edge functions as a razor. Wetting her toddler's hair with water, Washeman scraped a precise line across the boy's temple. "Maya is really good at this," she said, looking over at her mother.

"How many thousands of years," Possuelo asked, holding up the reed, "do you think it took them to develop this?"

By the water's edge, Maya whimpered from the malaria. We gave her quinine-based pills in water to drink each day. Next to her, Doni was sad-eyed and quiet. Recently, her baby died minutes after its birth.

A month after I left, Possuelo reported in a phone call, the Korubus watched an anaconda pull one of their children, a 3-year-old girl, underwater. Though they searched frantically, she never surfaced. The seventeen remaining tribespeople wept for her in the place she died, day after day.

And so lingering in my mind after my trip to the Javari rain forest was a question: Why preserve a life of hardship? But like gears in a machine, one question triggers the next. What kind of life would the modern world give them?

What the Future Holds

Possuelo, loving a good debate, argued that he was not defying destiny at all by trying to preserve the Indian way of life. There is nothing inevitable about Brazilian society swallowing up these hidden tribes, just as there was nothing preordained about humans landing on the moon, he said. Staking a nation's flag on a new frontier—whether on another planet or in the wilderness within your own borders—happens through deliberate policies that governments and people pursue.

But Possuelo could not have got this far on idealism alone. He is not naïve. As our journey neared its end, Possuelo acknowledged that however contact comes, the time that isolated tribes have left can probably be measured in decades. And time was precious, he said: not so much to prepare the Indians for contact, as to prepare the whites.

"Right now, the only door to our society that's open to the Indians is through the cellar," Possuelo said. Listen to the language of the settlers, he said, who call Indian lands "uninhabited," as if the natives did not exist. In nearly every case in which whites entered their lands, the Indians were reduced to scrounging for crumbs, as stores of fish, game, and timber vanished. Now, drug traffickers are trying to make inroads by building airstrips on their land. Funai's demarcation lines are designed not so much to keep the Indians confined to their ancient lands as to place a limit on white expansion, Possuelo said.

On the deck of the *Waika,* Possuelo traced the shape of the Javari Valley with his finger, much as the evening before he conjured figures as he gazed up at the clouds. It is true, he said, that the Javari is a rich, unspoiled area that could be developed.

"But why shouldn't the Indians be the ones to exploit it for themselves?" he asked. "Why shouldn't *they* be the ones selling their fish and game commercially?" It is a revolutionary thought in Brazil, where Indians have been virtually trained into dependence from their first moments of contact.

"I want to send Indians from here to school, have them steer our boats along the rivers," Possuelo said excitedly. Up and down the waterways, settlers are suffering through the malaria epidemic. He wanted to set up floating health stations for the river dwellers, run by the Indians. "Let the Indians be the ones drawing their blood, looking at it under the microscope, giving out the medications. Let the whites get used to seeing the Indians in positions of respect."

And that is the heart of Possuelo's dream, which more and more is coming to look like a plan: to turn the dark ecosystem of contact upside down, so that Indians may finally join Brazilian society standing tall. It is a vision he has peddled diligently, inviting small groups of reporters along on his expeditions to win public support, particularly overseas. Recently, the European Parliament awarded $1 million for a project Possuelo drew up to build health posts and provide education to Javari Valley tribes that had already been contacted by Funai officials. Idealist or not, Possuelo was sophisticated enough to apply for the grant through a private foundation—to prevent the money from getting siphoned into the Government's general coffers, or winding up in some politician's pocket. And his last expedition, for the Discovery Channel, carried a price: a 40-foot radio tower for the remote Javari Valley outpost.

But for all his savvy, Possuelo stands practically alone, in his own way isolated as much as the Indians he tracks. He, too, belongs to a vanishing breed. There are fewer than a dozen *sertanistas* in all of Brazil worthy of the name, he said, who did not get their titles as political rewards. And many of them would just as soon see his project disappear.

Indeed, it is impossible to imagine Possuelo's vision without Possuelo. What would have happened to the Government policy on isolated tribes if that car accident had ended his life or if his last boss had succeeded in firing him? Possuelo knows that his critics include not only industrialists, politicians, generals and academics but also fellow *sertanistas*. Like that of the anthropologists, their glory has always grown from presenting new cultures to the rest of the world, as if they had given birth to them. Yet as impossible as his quest may seem, Possuelo is determined to change peoples' minds. "I'm proposing the exact opposite," Possuelo said. "I say your glory is in *not* discovering them."

TIBETANS UNDER CHINESE RULE

Loretta Tofani

Since 1949 Tibet, a land noted for its distinctive Buddhist-based culture, has been occupied by the Chinese Communist government, which considers it a province of China. In the following article, Loretta Tofani, a staff writer for the *Philadelphia Inquirer,* reports that China's attempts to eradicate Tibet's religion and culture have included the imprisonment and torture of many Tibetans. China is also encouraging the resettlement of Chinese people into the region, with the intent of making Tibetans a minority in Tibet. Tofani writes that many people believe that China's actions constitute an example of cultural genocide—the destruction of Tibetans as a distinctive cultural group.

Each time the cattle prod stung her back with an electric current, Lobsang Choedon said, she could feel her skin "sizzle."

Then came electric shocks to her face, mouth, and arms.

Choedon was sixteen, a Buddhist nun, and she was being punished for a tiny act of defiance against the Chinese Communist government: On February 3, 1992, Choedon, in her burgundy robes, walked to the Jokhang, Tibet's most sacred temple, with five other young nuns. There, they prayed. Then they chanted these words: "Long live His Holiness the Dalai Lama. Independence for Tibet. Peace to the world."

Within minutes, Choedon was arrested. She said police threw her in a van, then beat her and kicked her with metal-toed boots. When she arrived at the jail, she said, police shocked her face, mouth, and arms repeatedly with a 7,000-volt cattle prod.

"Then I went numb," Choedon recalled in an interview in India, where she has lived since 1995. "Then the next day, all the pain hit me again."

She was sentenced without trial and served three years in prison. Three other nuns imprisoned with her also were tortured repeatedly, she said. They were not as fortunate as Choedon. They died after their torture—at ages 18, 19, and 24.

Excerpted from Loretta Tofani, "Bodies Scarred, Spirits Broken," *The Inquirer,* December 8, 1996. Reprinted with permission from *The Philadelphia Inquirer.*

A Campaign of Eradication

In Tibet, a land occupied by China since 1949, torture and intimidation are facts of life for Tibetans caught up in a Chinese campaign to eradicate Tibet's religion, nationality, and culture. In hundreds of interviews between 1994 and 1996, Tibetans have said Chinese police routinely arrest, jail, and torture people who question Chinese authority, even in the most mundane ways.

Tibet, known primarily for its Buddhism and scenic mountains, was invaded by China over a 10-year period beginning in 1949. The Tibetan government—headed by the nation's spiritual and political leader, the Dalai Lama—fled to exile in India in 1959, when China seized control of Lhasa, the capital.

Tibetans interviewed in India, Nepal, and Tibet said Chinese police and prison guards beat prisoners with chains, metal rods, and wooden sticks spiked with nails—usually while the victims are shackled or hanging from a ceiling. The most common instrument of torture, the Tibetans said, is the electric cattle prod, used in most countries to herd cows weighing up to 1,200 pounds. The police ram the prods into prisoners' mouths, rectums, and vaginas, according to Tibetans who have been imprisoned.

Their accounts have been verified by medical examinations and polygraph tests.

The former prisoners also report that police have held them in water while shocking them, branded their flesh with hot irons, kicked and beat them while they were on the ground, ordered trained dogs to attack and bite them, and locked them in concrete "coffins" for days or months at a time.

Virtually all Tibetans arrested for political reasons are tortured, according to interviews with hundreds of Tibetans, most of whom had been in prison.

China's official response to these findings was given by Lu Wen Xiang, first secretary in the press office of the Chinese Embassy in Washington: "This is not government policy. Chinese law forbids torture in jail. . . . I can't say this never happens. It depends on certain people."

China regards Tibet as part of China, saying China's activities there are an internal matter.

While atrocities in Bosnia and other countries command world attention, China has managed to keep the struggle in Tibet quiet. As the sole remaining superpower, the United States is the only nation with the political and economic leverage to pressure China into curbing human-rights abuses. It has condemned China's human-rights policies, but has not taken tough measures such as economic sanctions. . . .

The U.S. position on Tibet is divided. Congress passed a 1991 resolution calling Tibet an independent nation occupied by China; the U.S. State Department considers Tibet a part of China.

The United Nations also considers Tibet a part of China. The Dalai Lama has abandoned calls for full Tibetan independence and proposed that Tibet be granted autonomy over its domestic affairs while China controls defense and diplomatic issues. China has rejected the plan, and most Tibetans still insist on total independence.

Cultural Genocide

Human-rights groups have alleged for years that China has oppressed and killed Tibetans. The *Philadelphia Inquirer's* detailed and verified accounts of the experiences of political prisoners provide documentation of the torture. And Tibetans say China has embarked on a new phase of intimidation intended to eliminate the Buddhist faith and culture that has defined Tibet for centuries—and to extinguish all hopes of Tibetan independence.

"The Chinese are practicing cultural genocide in Tibet," the Dalai Lama said in an interview in Dharmsala, India.

Visits to Tibet and interviews with Tibetans show that Chinese oppression has intensified in several ways in recent years.

Tibetans are at times arrested for no stated reason, taken from their homes or places of work by Chinese police.

Authorities have forced teachers in Tibet to teach in Chinese. Usually, only one course is taught in Tibetan—Tibetan language.

They have forced out Tibetan shopkeepers and turned over their shops to Chinese merchants.

They have intensified efforts at "reeducation" by sending large contingents of Chinese soldiers into monasteries to interrogate every monk and nun individually about their allegiance to the Dalai Lama.

These interrogations are called "examinations." Those who refuse to renounce the Dalai Lama—which would be similar to a Christian denying Jesus Christ—are not allowed to remain in the monasteries. Some are jailed and tortured, Tibetans say.

According to monks in Lhasa, the Chinese have warned that they intend to one day extend the examinations to all Tibetans.

The Chinese also have forced monks to remove photos of the Dalai Lama from monasteries. When monks at Ganden Monastery resisted on May 7, 1996, police opened fire, wounding several and arresting dozens, according to relatives of Ganden monks.

Children in middle schools in Lhasa also were told in 1996 that they must not carry photos of the Dalai Lama or wear red cords that are blessed by a lama.

And thousands of Tibetans, imprisoned without due process, face torture and, in a few cases, death.

Like the Dalai Lama, more than 130,000 Tibetans have fled Tibet. Others continue to leave, most by taking a dangerous, two-week trek through the Himalayas, where the frozen bodies of other Tibetans who had attempted to escape are sometimes found embedded in ice along the trail, according to Tibetans who have made the journey.

China benefits economically and logistically from its control of Tibet. It takes lumber, gold, and uranium; it uses prisoners for mining and logging, according to former political prisoners. China also uses Tibet to test nuclear weapons and bury nuclear waste, despite Tibetans' opposition to nuclear weapons. Tibet is also a tourist attraction—especially for Buddhists and mountaineers—drawing millions of dollars every year, much of it enriching China's government. In addition, Tibet is an important military zone, sharing a border with India, Nepal, Bhutan, and Burma.

China has drastically changed Tibet's borders; much of what formerly was considered to be Tibet is now labeled as "Chinese provinces" on modern Chinese maps.

China's grip on Tibet is so tight that Lhasa, as well as much of the countryside, is patrolled by hundreds of thousands of Chinese soldiers and police. Undercover agents—posing as bicyclists, tourists, monks, businessmen—spy on Tibetans and visitors. The Chinese have paid some Tibetans to help spy and torture their countrymen.

Tibetans have not taken up arms. A pacifist people who practice Buddhism, Tibetans believe all living things are sacred. They do not believe in swatting flies, much less in attacking their enemies.

"We feel that our national struggle using the nonviolence principle is almost a new experiment on this planet," the Dalai Lama, who was awarded the Nobel Peace Prize in 1989, said in the 1996 interview in Dharmsala. "Of all the countries with problems in the world, only Tibet is responding with nonviolence, because life is sacred to Tibetans—even one life is important. The basic human nature is to have gentleness and compassion."

The Dalai Lama has become a thorn to the Chinese by traveling the world—from Hollywood to Paris—to focus attention on China's actions in Tibet.

Tibetan Prisoners

While China has destroyed thousands of Tibetan monasteries, businesses, and villages, it has built at least eighty-nine jails, detention centers, and other facilities where Tibetan dissidents are tortured. Today, there are 2,000 political prisoners in Tibet, according to various estimates. Virtually all of them have been tortured, former prisoners say.

Tibetans are being stunned with electricity, starved, and—occasionally—beaten to death, according to former prisoners. Since 1990, Amnesty International has documented the deaths of twenty-four Tibetans through torture. Between 1949 and 1979, Chinese authorities killed 1.2 million Tibetans, according to the Tibetan government in exile. Tibet's population before 1949 was six million.

The U.S. State Department says that "tens of thousands" of Tibetans were killed by the Chinese, "and close to 100,000 were imprisoned" during the 1950s.

"First they want to eliminate the monks and the nuns because we're politically active," said Jamphel Tsering, twenty-eight, a monk interviewed while trekking out of Tibet who said he was tortured repeatedly over five years. "Then they want to grind down the rest of the population. They're trying to destroy our whole culture and our belief system."

In interviews, Tibetans explained why they willingly took actions that would lead to certain torture.

"I feel angry," said Dawa Kyizom, a Tibetan student, now in India, who said she was tortured in jail after helping to make a Tibetan flag that was raised at a monastery. "The anger makes me have no fear. Most Tibetans have no fear. This is what makes us speak out for Tibetan independence and go to prison."

Lobsang Gyatso, a monk who has numerous wide scars on his stomach from torture, expressed a common sentiment—one steeped in Tibetan Buddhist religion and culture, which accepts suffering as part of life. When the police placed a burning hot shovel on his stomach, Gyatso said, "I thought, 'Whatever I'm suffering, I'm suffering for a cause. I have to suffer for the Tibetan people.' "

After a Chinese police officer repeatedly shocked Gyatso with an electric cattle prod, Gyatso felt another emotion typical of Tibetan Buddhists: compassion.

"I felt very sorry for the Chinese man," Gyatso said. "He had orders from the Chinese government to torture me. He would have lost his job if he didn't do it. The Chinese people are not so bad, but the government is very evil."

Chinese Migration

China has relocated 7.5 million Chinese to Tibet, according to studies commissioned by the Tibetan government in exile.

The country now houses more Chinese than Tibetans, who number 4.6 million. China offers economic incentives for working-class Chinese to emigrate to Tibet, while making it more difficult for ordinary Tibetans to earn a living.

Human-rights groups say that Tibetans own 25 percent of businesses in Lhasa, down from nearly 100 percent forty years ago.

In May 1993, Chinese officials said that massive Chinese migration into Tibet was successful. They termed it "the final solution."

"We are a minority in our own country," said Sonam Dolkar, twenty-five, a seamstress. "We are in our own country speaking a foreign language. It makes me very angry. There is no inner peace among Tibetans now."

Dolkar fled Tibet in 1992 with her daughter. They now live in India.

Over the years, China demolished virtually all of Tibet's 6,000 ancient monasteries and nunneries. At those that have been rebuilt, the number of monks and nuns continues to decline because of intensified enforcement of a quota imposed by the Chinese government.

At Drepung Monastery, the number of monks has fallen to about 500—from about 7,000 before the Chinese occupation.

"The Chinese have made my country into rags," said Tashi Lhundrup, twenty-nine, a monk who was jailed during a freedom demonstration. With scars on his ankles and wrists, he fled to Nepal in 1996 after being released from jail.

Torture Victims

The torture victims said that police sought "confessions" in which prisoners admitted they had written or said they wanted independence for Tibet. Police also demanded answers to questions like these: Isn't Tibet better off under Chinese rule? Don't you think you were wrong to challenge Chinese rule? Haven't you changed your mind about independence for Tibet?

Tibetans who had been arrested said that because of their strong beliefs, they answered the Chinese honestly, saying they wanted freedom for Tibet.

The result, they said, was usually hours of torture every day.

Relatively few political prisoners have trials or appear in courtrooms before judges. Most say they were simply handed a document in prison stating their sentence and crime—often "saying counterrevolutionary words." Some say they were simply released after being tortured for months, without being charged.

Because police are in charge of the prisons in Tibet, there is no separation of powers. The police and army officers who arrest citizens are the same people who deal with them in prison.

Nuns and monks are expelled from their nunneries and monasteries after they are arrested. When they get out of prison, they are forbidden by Chinese policy from rejoining their religious orders. As a result, many choose to leave their country and their families so they can practice their religion. Most of them have settled in India.

Laypeople who were political prisoners said they were unable to get jobs after being released from jail; they said their telephones are tapped by police; they and their families often are visited by police; and they are constantly followed by police. Therefore, many leave their country. . . .

Relations Between China and Tibet

China says that Tibet has always been a part of China, and that the 1949 occupation of Tibet was not illegal.

From 1908 to 1912, Tibet was under the influence of China. It also had been under the influence of Mongolia, Nepal, and Britain. There were also times in history in which Tibet had taken control of parts of China.

From 1913 to 1949, Tibet was an independent country. And for 2,000 years—despite the influence of outside forces at times—Tibet maintained its own government, its own small army, its own laws, its own currency, its own language, and its own culture. That started changing in 1949.

Physically, Tibetans and Chinese do not look alike; the Chinese recognized Tibetans in the past as a separate ethnic group. And while Tibet is an intensely religious country, most Chinese are atheists. (The government prefers atheism, and controls officially recognized religions.)

Before 1949, Tibet had conducted business with China and other nearby countries such as India, Nepal, and Japan.

The International Commission of Jurists, a Geneva-based association of judges and lawyers, ruled in 1960 that Tibet was an independent country before China invaded. The International Lawyers' Committee, another group of lawyers, reached the same conclusion in 1993.

The U.S. Congress also concluded, in a 1991 resolution, that Tibet is "an occupied country, under the established principles of international law."

The resolution, which was part of an authorization bill signed into law by President George Bush, said the legitimate representatives of Tibet are the Tibetan government in exile and the Dalai Lama.

Despite the resolution, the State Department has consistently said "U.S. policy is that Tibet is a part of China, and that recognition goes back historically."

China argues that it did not "invade" Tibet, but "liberated" it. In a "white paper," a government publication explaining its position, issued by China in 1992, China said that its intent has always been to bring "democratic reform" to Tibet. China said that before the "liberation," Tibetans lived in a "dark, feudal, exploitive society."

China said that Tibetan monks had been the "oppressors" who treated the rest of the Tibetan population as "serfs."

The Communist Chinese leader at the time of the invasion, Mao Tse-tung, called the religious culture of Tibet a "poison," a term he applied to all religions.

The Dalai Lama and the Tibetan government in exile say China's depiction of Tibet before 1949 is false, although they agree that the Tibetan government and society in 1949 needed reforms. However, they say, it was up to Tibet to decide on reforms, not China.

Cultural Collisions

Historically, Tibet's government—never a democracy—was a strange mix of Buddhist principles and brutality. Tibet was, and remains, a land where monasteries formed their own armies and where oracles were consulted on everything from rainfall to safe pilgrimages.

Heinrich Harrer, an Austrian who spent much of the 1940s in Tibet and wrote *Seven Years in Tibet*, found that all was calm and peaceful there, except for the treatment of convicted criminals.

Construction of buildings was often canceled because "worms and insects might easily be killed." But Tibet dealt with its criminals more harshly. Although the death penalty was forbidden, Harrer wrote, "theft and various minor offenses are punished with public whipping. . . . When highwaymen or robbers are caught they are usually condemned to have a hand or foot cut off."

Under China, Tibet has become a land of paradox: The children of nomads and city dwellers alike are expected to follow Communist doctrine; Tibetan language and math are being replaced by the Chinese system, even in the most remote villages. And the white scarves Tibetans give one another as a blessing are sold by Chinese merchants.

In Lhasa, where two cultures collide, rural pilgrims, dressed in sheepskin and fur hats, spin brass prayer wheels as they circumambulate the Potala, the former palace of the Dalai Lama. Across the street, Chinese soldiers in olive uniforms pose for pictures in front of a jet fighter. A mile away, Chinese prostitutes stroll the front of the Dalai Lama's former summer gardens. On the grounds, weeds are thick and the once splendid bamboo and stone residences have crumbled.

Some of the major religious and tourist areas of Lhasa, such as the Barkhor area, are constantly under the surveillance of video cameras attached to walls and columns. The Barkhor is the Tiananmen Square of Lhasa. In March of 1988, 18 demonstrating Tibetans were killed and 150 were wounded by Chinese officers. Some Tibetans had hurled rocks. The Dalai Lama subsequently renewed his pleas for nonviolence, and there have been few demonstrations since then in which Tibetans have done more than chant slogans.

Nagwang Rinchen, a 36-year-old monk, spent 6 and a half years in prison for carrying the Tibetan flag at a demonstration. He said he was tortured much of the time he was in jail; he was released in 1996.

"If things don't change, all that will be left of my country is the name, Tibet," Rinchen said. "The Chinese hold everything else. They've come into our country and now they're pushing us out from the middle."

CANADA'S CULTURAL GENOCIDE: FORCED REMOVAL OF NATIVE CHILDREN

Michael Downey

In the following article, Michael Downey describes a decades-long Canadian policy of removing indigenous children from their families. He explains that government child welfare agencies would regularly judge native parents to be unfit and would place their children in nonnative adoptive or foster families. Downey reports that many people now consider such policies to constitute cultural genocide because the children were purposefully removed from their culture and stripped of their language and sense of identity. Downey is a writer for *Maclean's*, a Canadian news magazine.

Carla Williams was four when the authorities knocked on the door and took the terrified Manitoba native youngster away from her parents forever. It was 1968, and Williams was thrust into a white society where nobody spoke her native tongue. Three years of cultural confusion later, she was adopted by a family that then moved to Holland. There the young girl was permitted no contact with her grieving parents back in Canada. Subjected to emotional and sexual abuse, she had three babies by the age of 16—two of them, she says, by her adoptive father, and one was given up for adoption. Finally, after her descent into alcohol, drugs, and prostitution, the Dutch government received an official request from Canada to have her returned. Williams left Amsterdam in 1989 at the age of 25, shouting, 'I'm going home!' She arrived back in Canada too late to meet the parents she had barely known: after the removal of three of their children, her native mother and father committed suicide.

Williams, now a saleswoman in Winnipeg, has had considerable success in turning her life around. But a 1999 study sheds light on a tragically disruptive program that saw thousands of young natives removed from their families for three decades starting in the 1950s. Children from native communities in British Columbia, Alberta, and Ontario as well as Manitoba were routinely shipped to nonnative foster homes or adoptive families far from their homes. Most of the 3,000 from Manitoba alone and many from the other provinces went to the United States, where placement agencies often received fees in the $15,000 to $20,000 range from the adoptive parents. One Manitoba judge has branded the child seizures 'cultural genocide,' and they do seem to fall well within the United Nations post-Second World War definition of genocide, which includes 'forcibly transferring children of [one] group to another group.'

The Sixties Scoop

In April 1999, after almost a year of hearings, a report will be delivered to the funding body, a joint committee of aboriginal groups and a unique partnership of four Ontario government ministries. Prepared by an aboriginal social agency, Native Child and Family Services of Toronto, and Toronto-based consultants Stevenato and Associates and Janet Budgell, the report is expected to examine the history of what authorities called the 'apprehensions' of native children, which continued into the early 1980s. The practice is sometimes referred to as the Sixties Scoop because the numbers peaked during that decade.

The seizures were carried out by child welfare agencies that insisted they were acting in the children's best interest—simply moving them into a better environment than they were getting in their native parents' home. Forced apprehensions of native children in fact began up to five generations earlier with the creation of residential schools, which functioned more as alternative parenting institutions than educational facilities. Those strict boarding schools effectively incarcerated native children for ten months of the year.

Unfortunately, many of the students returned from residential schools as distant, angry aliens, lacking emotional bonds with their own families. Having missed out on nurturing family environments, they were ill prepared to show affection or relate to their own children when they became parents—as most did at an early age. Then, in the 1950s and 1960s, the federal government delegated responsibility for First Nations health, welfare, and educational services to the provinces, while retaining financial responsibility for natives. With guaranteed payments from the federal government in Ottawa for each child apprehended, the number of First Nations children made wards of the state skyrocketed. In 1959, only 1 percent of Canadian children in custody were native; a decade later the number had risen to 40 percent, while aboriginals made up less than 4 percent of the population.

Ultimately, it became clear that the seizures were doing terrible damage to uncounted numbers of young natives. 'It was perhaps—perhaps—done with the best of intentions,' says David Langtry, current assistant deputy minister of Manitoba's child and family services. 'But once it became recognized that it was the wrong thing to do, changes were made to legislation.' A process introduced in 1988, he says, assures that an aboriginal child removed from a family will be placed in a new home according to strict priorities, turning to a non-native placement only as a last resort.

As previous investigations in other provinces have shown, the Sixties Scoop adoptions were rarely successful and many ended with children committing suicide. The Ontario report will undoubtedly refer to formal repatriation programs already in place in Manitoba and British Columbia—as well as Australia, where there was a similar seizure of aboriginals—with a view to helping others return to Canada, find their roots and locate their families. The study will also set the stage for new programs aimed at healing the collective native pain and perhaps, in time, the deep-rooted anger.

Tragic Stories

Individual stories of the Sixties Scoop paint a heart-wrenching picture. Sometimes, whole families of status and non-status Indian or Métis children were separated from each other, never to meet again. Names were changed, often several times. They were shipped thousands of kilometers from their people and denied contact with their parents, siblings, or communities or information about their heritage or culture. Some were enslaved, abused, and raped. And no Canadian body has ever officially taken responsibility, or apologized, for the policies.

Maclean's has learned that the new report will be soft on blame but frank about the extent of the tragedy still gripping native parents and plaguing the thousands of survivors who lost their names, language, families, childhood, and, above all, their identities. It will seek faster access to adoption records to speed repatriation. However, Sylvia Maracle, a member of the committee of the umbrella group that funded the study, says repatriations are only a partial remedy. 'We need to bring them back into the native circle,' she says, 'in a way that is comfortable for them.' The decision to commission the study recognized the bitterness felt by all native people, says Maracle, who is Mohawk. 'We are grieving,' she says, 'we are angry and we must do something to at least start the healing and in a holistic way.'

Joan Muir would agree. 'I was taken away from my family because my grandparents were alcoholics,' says the Vancouver resident, now 33, 'and placed with adoptive parents who were—as social workers had noted on my records prior to adoption—known alcoholics and racists.' Muir says she was raised to be ashamed of her native status. 'It just hit me a couple of years ago, that it's OK not to hide it anymore,' she says. 'Now that I'm away from my adoptive parents, I'm allowed to be native.'

The report will also refer to the tragic story of Richard Cardinal, a northern Alberta Métis forcibly removed from his family at age four. Over the next thirteen years, he was placed in twenty-eight homes and institutions. In one, he was beaten with a stick for wetting the bed. Another provided a bed just two feet wide in a flooded basement. One entire Christmas Day, while his adoptive family celebrated the holiday, Cardinal was kept outside in the cold, staring in. His suicide attempts began when he was nine. At his sixteenth foster home, aged 17, he nailed a board between two trees and hanged himself.

Toronto social worker Kenn Richard, a co-author of the report, says it outlines the history of the seizures through the words of people who experienced them firsthand. But he feels strongly that the practice was only one part of a long history of wrongheaded and disastrous policies towards Canada's native population. 'It's the legacy of child welfare in this country,' says Richard, 'that we have dysfunctional families and a deep anger among aboriginals.'

In the late '70s, Manitoba's native leaders rebelled against the permanent loss of their children. 'This was cultural genocide,' concluded Manitoba family court Judge Edwin Kimelman, called on to investigate the seizures in 1982. 'You took a child from his or her specific culture and you placed him into a foreign culture without any [counselling] assistance to the family which had the child. There's something drastically and basically wrong with that.' That year, Manitoba banned out-of-province adoptions of native children and overhauled its child welfare system. Native child welfare authorities were established across Canada.

Repairing the Damage

The task of repairing the damage is still under way. Lizabeth Hall, who grew up in a native family and now heads the British Columbia (B.C.) repatriation program, was shocked at the loss of identity among those removed from their native community. "People have called and asked, 'Can you just tell me what kind of Indian I am?" says Hall. "It made me cry. I'd like Canadians to know what happened and why. Non-natives always 'justify' their protection of natives; they don't realize the racism in that."

At a 1992 B.C. government hearing into the Sixties Scoop seizures, a First Nations elder addressed Canada's history of 'protecting' aboriginals. "For 30 years," said the elder, "generations of our children, the very future of our communities, have been taken away from us. Will they come home as our leaders, knowing the power and tradition of their people? Or will they come home broken and in pain, not knowing who they are, looking for the family that died of a broken heart?" Those are questions that new repatriation and education programs could help answer.

African Americans: Victims of Indirect Genocide

Robert Johnson and Paul S. Leighton

Robert Johnson is a professor of law, justice, and society at the American University in Washington, D.C. Paul S. Leighton is a professor specializing in prejudice and criminal justice policy at Eastern Michigan University in Ypsilanti. In the following essay, Johnson and Leighton contend that African Americans—particularly those of the underclass—are subjected to an indirect campaign of genocide. The authors concede that blacks in America do not face the same type of direct genocide experienced by the Jewish victims of the Holocaust. However, they argue that American social policies and entrenched racism condemn many blacks to impoverished and isolated ghettos. The stress created by such living conditions frequently results in self-destructive behavior that shortens the lives of African Americans, the authors conclude.

"Not since slavery," notes former U.S. Secretary of Human Services Dr. Louis Sullivan, "has so much calamity and ongoing catastrophe been visited on Black males." The calamities and catastrophes to which Dr. Sullivan alludes fall most heavily on poor black males, especially those who inhabit our nation's ghettos. Mortality data and other social indicators suggest that Dr. Sullivan's observation is fundamentally correct. These data suggest, moreover, that his claim can be extended to poor black women as well. We argue that the various calamities and castastrophes to which poor, inner-city African Americans are exposed reflect the operation of genocidal forces in their lives.

The Problem of Denial

The subject of genocide does not lend itself to forthright discussion. One distressing but recurrent problem is denial. Perpetrators of genocide may claim innocence even as bodies pile up around them. Prospective victims, not wanting to acknowledge the annihilation of their personal and collective identity, often participate directly or indirectly in their own demise. Trusting, some follow authorities to the ends of their lives; others, suffused with self-loathing, destroy their

Excerpted from Robert Johnson and Paul S. Leighton, "American Genocide: The Destruction of the Black Underclass," in *Collective Violence: Harmful Behavior in Groups and Governments*, edited by Craig Summers and Eric Markusen. Copyright © 1999 Rowman & Littlefield Publishers, Inc. Reprinted with permission from The University Press of America.

own lives or those of their fellows, doing the devil's work with malevolent abandon. Scholars have been largely out of touch with the realities of genocide. "Our review of the history of genocide and its neglect," note Frank Chalk and Kurt Jonassohn, "has led us to the conclusion that until very recently scholars participated in a process of pervasive and self-imposed denial."

Countering the forces of denial is a more recent tendency for accusations of genocide to become shorthand expressions of general moral condemnation. In this sense, genocide is not denied but seen everywhere. We read of economic and educational genocide, with bad jobs or poor schools depicted as lethal enterprises. The French charge the Euro-Disney amusement park with cultural genocide, as if Mickey Mouse could destroy French culture with a swipe of his tail. Such fanciful usages empty the term of moral currency.

The claim that underclass African Americans are victims of genocide has not been assessed in dispassionate terms. White scholars have essentially ignored the issue; others pause only to label such beliefs a species of lunacy. An earlier black scholar named William Patterson formally charged the United States with the genocide of blacks before the United Nations during the 1950s, but he has been largely forgotten. Later black writers who have tackled the issue at any length have done so with little reference to the body of research on genocide.

There can be no doubt that many African Americans believe that the more marginal members of the black community, if not all black Americans, have been and remain today actual or potential targets of genocide. Some state these beliefs quite bluntly, decrying conspiratorial plans to annihilate the black race. Such claims are typically seen as nothing less than bizarre. In the words of a *Newsweek* writer, Lorene Cary, "The ideological wagons are drawn into a circle with sensible mainstream American reason inside, threatened but valiant, and the crazy assault of black-American paranoia without." Indeed, a 1990 article in *U.S. News & World Report* was entitled, "The Return of the Paranoid Style in American Politics." The aim of the article was revealed in the subtitle, which read in part, "why some blacks . . . fear 'genocide.'"

We find it significant that the term *paranoid* was used literally (without quotations) while the term *genocide* was used figuratively (within quotes). The implication is that one must be crazy—a purveyor of so much "mumbo jumbo," in the words of noted *Time* writer Jack White—to think that some black Americans are victims of genocide. We contend that it is entirely possible that the paranoia alluded to is figurative and the feared genocide literal. Poor, inner-city African Americans are subjected to many disabling conditions, most notably poverty and racism but also the widespread and demoralizing perception that they are victims of a host of conspiracies, from the introduction of drugs and AIDS into their communities to the larger threat of genocide. It is of course true that the fate of underclass black Americans is not that of the death camp and institutionalized slaughter. Nevertheless, our assessment of the evidence leads us to conclude that their plight goes beyond simple political oppression and crosses the threshold of genocide.

Dimensions of Genocide

We suspect that many people believe that claims of black genocide are, to put it charitably, overstated if not overwrought, much as Mark Twain once claimed rumors of his death were greatly exaggerated. We suspect this because the implicit definition of genocide held by most people is informed by the Nazi Holocaust. In this view, genocide necessarily entails direct and sustained and highly organized violence of a most gruesome and cold-blooded sort. Surely, reasonable people contend, black Americans are not suffering a hidden holocaust in our midst!

But a Nazi-inspired definition of genocide is misleading. The Holocaust represents the extreme or limiting case of genocide, not the paradigm, just as a rape-murder-disembowelment represents the extreme or limiting case of murder, not a typical or representative example of homicide. So what is genocide if not one holocaust or another?

There is, in fact, no single, formal definition of genocide that shares widespread acceptance. The most commonly cited definition, found in the United Nations Genocide Convention, is as much the result of political wrangling in the fledgling United Nations as it is the product of academic or theoretical analysis. In our view, the best definition is one offered by Ervin Staub. Drawing on a wide-ranging study of the subject, Staub defines genocide as "an attempt to exterminate a racial, ethnic, religious, cultural, or political group, either directly through murder or indirectly by creating conditions that lead to the group's destruction."

To be sure, terms such as *exterminate* harken back to the Holocaust, and bring to mind Nazi death camps replete with ovens and gas chambers as settings of mass execution. But a careful reading of Staub's definition makes clear that: (1) most genocide efforts amount to "attempts" to destroy a group rather than complete success at a group's annihilation—the Nazis, for example, failed to eliminate the Jews or indeed any of the other populations they targeted for extermination; (2) attempts at genocide span direct violence (murder) as well as indirect violence (primarily systematic deprivation); and (3) genocide is expressed in high mortality rates and/or high rates of other disabilities that threaten to destroy the group. Critically, then, the key concept at the core of the notion of genocide is the attempted destruction of a group—an end that can be pursued in various ways.

As Staub explains, "The essence of evil is the destruction of human beings." Destruction encompasses "not only killing but creation of conditions that materially or psychologically destroy or diminish people's dignity, happiness, and capacity to fulfill basic material needs." The notion that genocide need not entail direct physical violence is reinforced by Raphael Lemkin, who coined the term *genocide*—from the Greek work *genos* (race or tribe) and the Latin *cide* (kill)—and helped draft the U.N. Genocide Convention. His 1944 work, while explicitly referring to nations and national groups, is equally applicable to racial and ethnic groups. At the heart of genocide, Lemkin contends, are undertakings that have as their goal the "destruction of the essential foundations of the life" of the group. This destruction can be sought by direct means (where the goal is "immediate destruction") or by indirect means (where the goal is "disintegration"). In either case, the integrity of the group's basic institutions is compromised, producing in varying degrees the "destruction of the personal security, liberty, health, dignity, and even the lives of the individuals belonging to such groups."

Indirect Genocide

The imposition of destructive life conditions amounts to genocide when those conditions undermine the group's existence and substantially damage the lives of its members. For purposes of clarity, we call this indirect genocide, to distinguish it from direct genocide of the sort typified by the Nazi Holocaust. Indirect genocide proceeds by methods that are slower and less spectacular than death camps, but this insidious approach has advantages over more direct violence. Several instances of man-made famine have resulted in genocide. These famines are man-made in the sense that they were created or tolerated as a matter of policy. The Irish potato famine is a case in point. Policies set in England resulted in shortages of food in Ireland; starvation, aided by diseases that ran rampant due to malnutrition, terminated Irish lives on a large scale. Throughout, destructive policies were left in place by the British authorities.

Indirect genocide such as that which occasioned the Irish potato famine, Jonassohn writes, "combines advantages—for the perpetrators—of costing very little while at the same time putting physical distance between them and the victims." Physical distance, in turn, can translate into psychological distance, creating a mental or emotional buffer protecting the perpetrators of violence from full recognition of the consequences of their actions. Cues to human suffering—vacant stares, distended bellies, atrophied limbs—would almost certainly promote empathy for victims and hence distress among the perpetrators, but they are hidden from the victimizer. This buffering or protective effect also reflects a discontinuity between the perpetrator's acts—policy decisions rendered in the comfort of an office—and the victims' agonizing deaths from starvation. One's actions cause suffering vastly out of proportion to one's intent. Denial can come easily in this context.

One can readily ignore the suffering of others, especially others whose plight is hidden from view, and remain secure in the belief that one's actions—including one's inaction—can't possibly have had such drastic consequences for others.

For those who do attend to the suffering, the situation can be readily mistaken for something less morally odious than genocide. Life is unfair, we might maintain. Famines happen. Who are we to change the course of human affairs? We hold such views with apparent stoicism, as long as we are not the victims of life's unfairness, and can go about the business of reaping the benefits of our privileged positions. Good camouflage for indirect genocide is provided by prejudice and our desire to believe that bad things do not happen to good people. If a group suffers greatly, so the logic runs, they must in some sense deserve their ugly fate. If the group is a despised racial minority, it is easy to conclude, harkening back to Dr. Sullivan's observation, that they brought down upon themselves the various calamities and catastrophes that mar their bleak lives.

We will return to the topic of belief and ideology when we discuss genocidal intent. The important point here is that if creating or tolerating a famine can be genocidal, there is no reason why the same principle does not apply to creating or tolerating *multiple* destructive life conditions. In the inner cities of the United States, we argue, the interaction of poverty and racism produces social pathologies that undermine the essential foundations of group life in underclass African American communities. These impoverished ghettos are, ultimately, the responsibility of the larger white society. As noted in the National Advisory Commission on Civil Disorders,

> What white Americans have never fully understood—but what the Negro can never forget—is that white society is deeply implicated in the ghetto. White institutions created it, white institutions maintain it, and white society condones it.

It is fair to say that the larger white society has, in effect, imprisoned poor blacks in these isolated environments, then turned its back on these captives so as not to fully comprehend the suffering and death that are the hallmarks of ghetto life.

The conditions of life in American black ghettos are objectively destructive. Poverty and attendant social ills that plague these communities tear at the fabric of group life, creating a genocidal environment. Genocide may also occur through self-destructive adaptations to the dysfunctional life conditions presented by such pathological environments. The link between policy and outcome remains but is less obvious. In American ghettos, for example, poverty and racism rarely kill directly. Few people drop dead in the streets from hunger or exposure to the elements, and few die from direct violence whose immediate impetus is virulent racism. But the effects of poverty and racism are widespread, and produce a range of physical and psychological stresses. Some reactions to these stresses are expressed in behaviors that destroy life. Thus, destruction need not come only from outside of the group. Members of the victim group may contribute to their own victimization through adaptations to bleak life conditions that include direct violence aimed at others in the group (e.g., homicide), as well as indirect violence in the form of self-destructive lifestyles, notably addiction to drugs and alcohol, that foreshorten the lives of group members.

The Role of Self-Destruction

Chancellor Williams, in his classic *Destruction of Black Civilization*, writes of genocide emanating from within the black community:

> They, the so-called criminals and their youthful followers, expect nothing beneficial from the white world, and they see no reason for hope in their own. Hence, like caged animals, they strike at what is nearest them—their own people. They are actually trying to kill a situation they hate, unaware that even in this, they are serving the white man well. For the whites need not go all out for "genocide" schemes, for which they are often charged, when blacks are killing themselves off daily on such a large scale.

Andrew Hacker picks up on this critical theme, characterizing the violent and other destructive behaviors of young black men as "self-inflicted genocide" in the face of a white society marked by a racial caste system that "imposes a stigma on every black child at birth."

In the context of self-inflicted genocide, the victim group appears to be the primary if not exclusive cause of its own problems. Any role played by larger social conditions is readily discounted or even ignored entirely. It is commonly said, for example, that blacks are killing themselves with guns and drugs. Other sources of increased mortality in the black community, such as those related to poor physical health, can be dismissed on the same grounds. The culprit is *their* diet or lifestyle. In our view, these choices reflect adaptations to a broader social context marked by a "socioeconomic predicament which is itself profoundly antisocial," in the words of R.L. Rubenstein. Violence and drug abuse are not overrepresented in American ghettos by chance, as though these settings of poverty were merely neutral staging grounds for destructive behavior. Ghettos, instead, are brutal and indeed antisocial environments that, through the pressures they offer, promote a host of destructive adaptations to daily life. Thus, the refrain, "they kill themselves," must be met with the rejoinder, "but society sets the stage for that violence." Here, society means white society. As Hacker has succinctly put it, "It is white America that has made being black so disconsolate an estate."

Genocidal conditions exert a powerful influence on behavior. Victims may collude in their victimization, even in the extreme case of direct genocide represented by the Holocaust. Hannah Arendt is quite blunt in discussing

> the submissive meekness with which Jews went to their death—arriving on time at the transportation points, walking on their own feet to the places of execution, digging their own graves, undressing and making neat piles of their clothing, and lying down side by side to be shot.

The Holocaust literature also raises questions about whether the Jewish Councils, the putative representatives of the doomed communities, were in fact vehicles of genocide because of their ties with the Nazis and their ability to organize the Jewish communities in ways that served the ends of their oppressors.

Even if the worst of Arendt's accusations are true, they do not change the essential meaning of the Holocaust. In the case of blacks in the United States, the point is illustrated by a discussion posted on one of the many racist Internet sites. In this posting, a "theorist" (writing "in loyal service to the white race") explored the idea of legalizing crack cocaine and having the government give it out free. Under this plan, blacks could smoke all they wanted, but only at one place, "because if you didn't keep them there they'd be dying all over and they'd be stinking and you'd have to pay someone to go find them. It would be cheaper if you just kept them there and dug a big ditch out back to bury them." A person identified as "The Aryan Crusader" responded, "it kind of sounds like another holocaust to me . . . I ain't saying it's wrong, I'm just saying that it sounds like another holocaust."

The self-proclaimed Aryan Crusader is of course right. This plan is "like another Holocaust." The lack of explicit coercion—the lack of a "gun to their head," as many would say—does not change the fundamental nature of these dynamics. When people face genocidal pressures, some degree of maladaptive behavior is normal—or at least to be expected, given the stresses of the situation. A caveat is in order here. To identify genocidal conditions as sources of destructive behavior is not to exonerate the offending individuals for their behavior. As a general rule, victims who victimize others in turn remain culpable for their actions, though that culpability is reduced or mitigated by the considerable pressures that circumscribe their lives. Jeffrey Reiman makes this point quite clearly in the context of poverty and crime. "To point to the unique social pressures that lead the poor to prey on one another is to point to a mitigating, not an excusing, factor. Even the victims of exploitation and oppression have moral obligations not to harm those who do not exploit them or who share their oppression." Indeed, even the victims of virtually unparalleled exploitation and oppression in the Nazi death camps held each other accountable to a moral code that prohibited abusing fellow suffers.

Several factors, some noted earlier, make it difficult to appreciate the dynamics of indirect genocide as they apply to African Americans. The larger white society is quite removed from the grim life circumstances shared by underclass blacks and hence the typical white American has little real feeling for the forces that shape their lives. In our remote ghettos, death flows not from gas chambers and state-sponsored torture, but from lives of deprivation and desperation that are unfathomable to outsiders. The relative subtlety of this process—combining an isolated location and a subtle and complex causal chain—helps explain why blacks can sincerely assert claims of genocide and whites, just as sincerely, can assert their innocence and moral goodness.

At bottom, many whites suppose that since they do not desire or intend the extermination of African Americans, genocide cannot happen—by definition or in practice. This disclaimer is inadequate because it does not capture the complexities of intent and belief in the context of indirect genocide.

Intent and Belief

Most readers would agree that conditions for inner-city blacks create extreme misery and foreshortened lives—or at least would find that information believable if it were made available to them—yet they would argue that we as a society do not intend that those conditions exist let alone that they result in extermination. Few Americans explicitly condone racism, though racist views, featuring beliefs about white supremacy, are disturbingly common. Even fewer still could be said to desire in any conscious way the extermination of blacks. We would agree, further, that there is little credible evidence to suggest the existence of an overt plot or a conspiracy to destroy African Americans. As Reiman suggests,

> conspiracy theories are not plausible because they do not correspond to the way most people act most of the time. Although there is no paucity of conscious mendacity and manipulation in our politics, most people most of the time seem sincerely to believe that what they are doing is right.

No definition of genocide requires a conspiracy to prove the element of intent. (Conspiracies are discussed most frequently by those who wish to discredit the claim of genocide.) Images of a diabolical plot presided over by a nefarious white power elite are easy to dismiss as paranoid, and those who charge genocide are thus readily portrayed as "wild-eyed conspiracy mongers," in the words of White. Denial of genocide is made easy by dispatching such straw man arguments.

Some notion of intent is "essential" to establish genocide, note Chalk and Jonassohn, "in order to exclude those cases in which the outcome was neither planned nor predicted." Excluded cases of mass destruction would include both "natural disasters" and "mass deaths that were the result of some human action that did not have this intent (for example, the spread of diseases as a result of migration)" and could not reasonably be foreseen or prevented.

Genocide thus requires human action that is not accidental. The destruction of groups needs to be, at minimum, predictable, though it could also be the desired result of concerted effort (literally, a conspiracy). The broader use of the term *intentional* suggests an awareness for which perpetrators are culpable because they fail to act to prevent harms that, though not intended, can be foreseen as the outcome of their actions. Philosopher R.M. Hare elaborates on this aspect of intentionality:

> There is a distinction, important for some purposes, between direct and oblique intention. To intend some consequence directly one has to desire it. To intend it obliquely one has only to foresee it. . . . We have the duty to avoid bringing about consequences that we ought not bring about, even if we do not desire those consequences in themselves, provided only that we know they will be consequences. I am to blame if I knowingly bring about someone's death in the course of some plan of mine, even if I do not desire his death in itself— that is, even if I intend the death only obliquely and not directly. As we shall see, this is very relevant to the decisions of legislators (many of whose intentions are oblique), in that they have a duty to consider consequences of their legislation that they can foresee, and not merely those that they desire.

Genocide is undoubtedly a "consequence we ought not bring about," to quote Hare, so the desire to destroy a group is less relevant than whether that destruction can be foreseen or predicted. Genocide thus requires only indirect or oblique intent for culpability, though direct intent does create a higher degree of culpability. Those who foresee and fail to act are less culpable than those who plan and carry out a harmful act or plan of action. However, once harmful consequences come to pass, they are matters of fact, not prediction. If known consequences are not acted on, indirect intent is made direct. In the face of evidence of genocide, as Roger Smith states, "to persist" with destructive policies "is to intend the death of a people."

APPENDIX

The Convention on the Prevention and Punishment of the Crime of Genocide

The Genocide Convention was adopted by the United Nations on December 9, 1948. It entered into force on January 12, 1951, following its ratification by twenty member nations. The United States formally joined the Convention in 1988.

The Contracting Parties, having considered the declaration made by the General Assembly of the United Nations in its resolution 96 (I) dated 11 December 1946 that genocide is a crime under international law, contrary to the spirit and aims of the United Nations and condemned by the civilized world, recognizing that at all periods of history genocide has inflicted great losses on humanity, and being convinced that, in order to liberate mankind from such an odious scourge, international co-operation is required, hereby agree as hereinafter provided:

Article 1

The Contracting Parties confirm that genocide, whether committed in time of peace or in time of war, is a crime under international law which they undertake to prevent and to punish.

Article 2

In the present Convention, genocide means any of the following acts committed with intent to destroy, in whole or in part, a national, ethnical, racial or religious group, as such:

(a) Killing members of the group;
(b) Causing serious bodily or mental harm to members of the group;
(c) Deliberately inflicting on the group conditions of life calculated to bring about its physical destruction in whole or in part;
(d) Imposing measures intended to prevent births within the group;
(e) Forcibly transferring children of the group to another group.

Article 3

The following acts shall be punishable:

(a) Genocide;
(b) Conspiracy to commit genocide;
(c) Direct and public incitement to commit genocide;
(d) Attempt to commit genocide;
(e) Complicity in genocide.

Article 4

Persons committing genocide or any of the other acts enumerated in article III shall be punished, whether they are constitutionally responsible rulers, public officials or private individuals.

Article 5

The Contracting Parties undertake to enact, in accordance with their respective Constitutions, the necessary legislation to give effect to the provisions of the present Convention, and, in particular, to provide effective penalties for persons guilty of genocide or any of the other acts enumerated in article III.

Article 6

Persons charged with genocide or any of the other acts enumerated in article III shall be tried by a competent tribunal of the State in the territory of which the act was committed, or by such international penal tribunal as may have jurisdiction with respect to those Contracting Parties which shall have accepted its jurisdiction.

Article 7

Genocide and the other acts enumerated in article III shall not be considered as political crimes for the purpose of extradition.

The Contracting Parties pledge themselves in such cases to grant extradition in accordance with their laws and treaties in force.

Article 8

Any Contracting Party may call upon the competent organs of the United Nations to take such action under the Charter of the United Nations as they consider appropriate for the prevention and suppression of acts of genocide or any of the other acts enumerated in article III.

Article 9

Disputes between the Contracting Parties relating to the interpretation, application or fulfilment of the present Convention, including those relating to the responsibility of a State for genocide or for any of the other acts enumerated in article III, shall be submitted to the International Court of Justice at the request of any of the parties to the dispute.

Article 10

The present Convention, of which the Chinese, English, French, Russian and Spanish texts are equally authentic, shall bear the date of 9 December 1948.

Article 11

The present Convention shall be open until 31 December 1949 for signature on behalf of any Member of the United Nations and of any nonmember State to which an invitation to sign has been addressed by the General Assembly.

The present Convention shall be ratified, and the instruments of ratification shall be deposited with the Secretary-General of the United Nations.

After 1 January 1950, the present Convention may be acceded to on behalf of any Member of the United Nations and of any non-member State which has received an invitation as aforesaid. Instruments of accession shall be deposited with the Secretary-General of the United Nations.

Article 12

Any Contracting Party may at any time, by notification addressed to the Secretary-General of the United Nations, extend the application of the present Convention to all or any of the territories for the conduct of whose foreign relations that Contracting Party is responsible.

Article 13

On the day when the first twenty instruments of ratification or accession have been deposited, the Secretary-General shall draw up a proces-verbal and transmit a copy thereof to each Member of the United Nations and to each of the non-member States contemplated in article 11.

The present Convention shall come into force on the ninetieth day following the date of deposit of the twentieth instrument of ratification or accession.

Any ratification or accession effected, subsequent to the latter date shall become effective on the ninetieth day following the deposit of the instrument of ratification or accession.

Article 14

The present Convention shall remain in effect for a period of ten years as from the date of its coming into force.

It shall thereafter remain in force for successive periods of five years for such Contracting Parties as have not denounced it at least six months before the expiration of the current period.

Denunciation shall be effected by a written notification addressed to the Secretary-General of the United Nations.

Article 15

If, as a result of denunciations, the number of Parties to the present Convention should become less than sixteen, the Convention shall cease to be in force as from the date on which the last of these denunciations shall become effective.

Article 16

A request for the revision of the present Convention may be made at any time by any Contracting Party by means of a notification in writing addressed to the Secretary-General.

The General Assembly shall decide upon the steps, if any, to be taken in respect of such request.

Article 17

The Secretary-General of the United Nations shall notify all Members of the United Nations and the non-member States contemplated in article XI of the following:

(a) Signatures, ratifications and accessions received in accordance with article 11;

(b) Notifications received in accordance with article 12;

(c) The date upon which the present Convention comes into force in accordance with article 13;

(d) Denunciations received in accordance with article 14;

(e) The abrogation of the Convention in accordance with article 15;

(f) Notifications received in accordance with article 16.

Article 18

The original of the present Convention shall be deposited in the archives of the United Nations.

A certified copy of the Convention shall be transmitted to each Member of the United Nations and to each of the non-member States contemplated in article XI.

Article 19

The present Convention shall be registered by the Secretary-General of the United Nations on the date of its coming into force.

ORGANIZATIONS TO CONTACT

Center for Holocaust and Genocide Studies (CHGS)
University of Minnesota
100 Nolte Hall West, 315 Pillsbury Dr., Minneapolis, MN 55455
(612) 626-2235 • fax: (612) 626-9169
e-mail: chgs@tc.umn.edu • website: www.chgs.umn.edu

Sponsored by the University of Minnesota, CWGS works in conjunction with university departments and off-campus organizations to provide educational resources to teachers, the media, and others interested in the study and teaching of the Holocaust and other genocides. It publishes the *CHGS Newsletter* twice a year and maintains a website with an extensive listing of bibliographic materials.

Center for World Indigenous Studies (CWIS)
1001 Cooper Pt. Rd. SW, Suite 140-214, Olympia, WA 98502
(360) 754-1990
e-mail: usaoffice@cwis.org • website: www.cwis.org

CWIS is an independent research and education organization that concentrates on the political, social, and economic status of indigenous peoples. It publishes the newsletter *Fourth World Eyes*. Its website includes numerous position statements and reports on the cultural genocide of indigenous peoples.

Centre for Comparative Genocide Studies (CCGS)
Department of Politics, Macquarie University, NSW, 2109, Australia
(61) 2 9850-8822 • fax: (61) 2 9850-8240
website: www.genocide.mq.edu.au/ccgs.htm

CCGS sponsors ongoing research on aspects of genocide in Africa, Bosnia, East Timor, and other regions of the world. Among its publications are a quarterly newsletter and the book *Genocide Perspectives*.

Coalition for International Justice
740 15th St NW, 8th Fl., Washington, DC 20005-1009
(202) 662-1595 • fax: (202) 662-1597
e-mail: jheffernan@cij.org • website: www.cij.org

The coalition works to support the Yugoslavia and Rwanda war crimes tribunals through advocacy, fundraising, and technical legal assistance. It created War Criminal Watch to track and publicize the criminal acts of suspected war criminals in Rwanda and the former Yugoslavia. On its website, it publishes dossiers on indicted suspects and provides links to news articles.

Cultural Survival
215 Prospect St., Cambridge, MA 02139
(617) 441-5400 • fax: (617) 441-5417
website: www.cs.org

Founded in 1972, Cultural Survival is an international advocate for the human rights and self-determination of indigenous peoples. It publishes *Cultural Survival Quarterly*.

Human Rights Watch (HRW)
350 Fifth Ave., 34th Fl., New York, NY 10018-3299
(212) 290-4700 • fax: (212) 736-1300
e-mail: hrwnyc@hwr.org • website: www.hrw.org

HRW is an international organization committed to defending human rights. It investigates and reports on genocide and other human rights violations around the world and seeks to hold violators accountable for their actions. It publishes the annual *Human Rights Watch World Report* as well as special regional reports, including "Leave None to Tell the Story: Genocide in Rwanda."

Montreal Institute for Genocide and Human Rights Studies (MIGS)
Concordia University
1455 De Maisonneuve Blvd. West, Montreal, Quebec, H3G 1M8 Canada
(514) 848-2404 • fax: (514) 848-4538
e-mail: migs@concordia.ca • website: www.migs.org

Based out of the history and sociology departments of Concordia University, the institute collects and disseminates research into the historical origins of genocides and mass killings. MIGS publishes periodic research papers on genocide. Its website includes links to editorial articles on genocide and memoirs of Holocaust survivors.

Prevent Genocide International (PGI)
1804 S St. NW, Washington, DC 20009
(202) 483-1948 • fax: (202) 328-0627
e-mail: info@preventgenocide.org • website: www.preventgenocide.org

Founded in 1998, PGI is a global, Internet-based network of activists working to prevent the crime of genocide. Its website contains the text of laws concerning genocide in the criminal codes of twelve nations and in international law. It also presents selected writings of Raphael Lemkin, originator of the word "genocide."

Simon Wiesenthal Center
9760 W. Pico Blvd., Los Angeles, CA 90035
(310) 553-9036 • fax: (310) 553-8007
e-mail: webmaster@wiesenthal.com • website: www.wiesenthal.com

The center maintains offices throughout the world in the interest of fighting against bigotry and anti-semitism. Its primary activities include Holocaust remembrance and the defense of human rights. The center's Museum of Tolerance in Los Angeles showcases multimedia exhibits and maintains an information resource center on the Holocaust and other twentieth-century genocides. The center publishes *Response* magazine quarterly.

United Nations (UN)
United Nations Publications
Two UN Plaza, DC2-856, New York, NY 10017
(212) 963-5455 • fax: (212) 963-4116
e-mail: lubomudrov@un.org • website: www.un.org

An organization of sovereign nations, the UN's purpose is to help find solutions to international problems and disputes. The organization publishes the quarterly *UN Chronicles* as well as reports on genocide and other human rights issues. Its website contains the texts of international law treaties, information on the International Criminal Court, and reports concerning genocide.

United States Institute of Peace (USIP)
1200 17th St. NW, Suite 200, Washington, DC 20036-3011
(202) 457-1700 • fax: (202) 429-6063
e-mail: usip_requests@usip.org • website: www.usip.org

An independent, nonpartisan federal institution, the United States Institute of Peace promotes the peaceful resolution of international conflicts. It seeks to educate the public about international peacemaking efforts through publications, electronic outreach, workshops, and conferences. USIP's publications include the bimonthly newsletter *Peace Watch* and the report "Rwanda: Accountability for War Crimes and Genocide."

U.S. Committee for Refugees (USCR)
1717 Massachusetts Ave. NW, Suite 200, Washington, DC 20036
(202) 347-3507 • fax: (202) 347-3418
e-mail: uscr@irsa-uscr.org • website: www.refugees.org

USCR works to protect and assist refugees worldwide, including those fleeing ethnic violence and genocidal situations. It also documents and reports conditions faced by refugees, displaced persons, and people seeking asylum. The committee publishes the annual *UCSR World Refugee Survey*, monthly refugee reports, and issue papers such as "Left After Death: Suspicion and Reintegration in Post-Genocide Rwanda."

The World Federalist Association (WFA)
418–420 7th St. SE, Washington, DC 20003
(202) 546-3950 • fax: (202) 546-3749
e-mail: info@endgenocide.org • website: www.endgenocide.org

The World Federalist Association consists of individuals and nongovernmental organizations who work together to strengthen and reform the United Nations and to apply the rule of law to global problems, including genocide. WFA publishes *World Federalist,* a quarterly newsletter. It also sponsors the Campaign to End Genocide, a multi-organizational effort to promote measures to prevent future genocides, such as the creation of a UN rapid response force.

Internet Resources

Crimes of War Project
www.crimesofwar.org

This website is part of a collaborative effort of journalists, lawyers, and scholars to raise public awareness concerning the prevention and punishment of genocide and other aspects of international humanitarian law. It presents definitions of key legal terms and examines events in Bosnia, Rwanda, and other current armed conflicts.

Cybrary of the Holocaust
http://remember.org/index.html

This website collects and disseminates educational materials related to the Holocaust.

Genocide Research Project
www.people.memphis.edu/~genocide/

The Genocide Research Project (GRP), a joint endeavor of the University of Memphis and Pennsylvania State University, is a collaborative effort of academic scholars to encourage research on genocide and to educate the public on issues concerning genocide. Its website features an annotated bibliography of published materials on genocide and links to other websites related to the study of genocide.

Web Genocide Documentation Centre

www.ess.uwe.ac.uk/genocide/genocide.htm

Created by Dr. Stuart Stein of the University of the West of England, this website provides continually updated links to historical articles and primary source documents on twentieth-century genocides.

BIBLIOGRAPHY

Books

Beverly Allen	*Rape Warfare: The Hidden Genocide in Bosnia-Herzegovina and Croatia.* Minneapolis: University of Minnesota Press, 1996.
George J. Andreopoulos	*Genocide: Conceptual and Historical Dimensions.* Philadelphia: University of Pennsylvania Press, 1994.
Michael Burleigh	*Ethics and Examination: Reflections on Nazi Genocide.* New York: Cambridge University Press, 1997.
Israel W. Charny, ed.	*Encyclopedia of Genocide.* Santa Barbara, CA: ABC-Clio, 1999.
Levon Chorbajian and George Shirinian, eds.	*Studies in Comparative Genocide.* New York: St. Martin's Press, 1999.
Ward Churchill	*A Little Matter of Genocide: Holocaust and Denial in the Americas, 1492 to the Present.* San Francisco: City Lights, 1997.
Norman Cigar	*Genocide in Bosnia: The Policy of "Ethnic Cleansing" in Eastern Europe.* College Station: Texas A & M University Press, 1995.
Vahakn N. Dadrian	*The History of the Armenian Genocide: Ethnic Conflict from the Balkans to Anatolia to the Caucasus.* Providence, RI: Berghahn Books, 1997.
Bruce Elder	*Blood on the Wattle: Massacres and Maltreatment of Aboriginal Australians Since 1788.* Sydney, Australia: New Holland Books, 1999.
Henry Friedlander	*The Origins of Nazi Genocide: From Euthanasia to the Final Solution.* Chapel Hill: University of North Carolina Press, 1995.
Ina R. Friedman	*The Other Victims: First-Person Stories of Non-Jews Persecuted by the Nazis.* New York: Houghton Mifflin, 1995.
Roy Gutman	*A Witness to Genocide: The 1993 Pulitzer Prize-winning Dispatches on the "Ethnic Cleansing" of Bosnia.* New York: Macmillan, 1993.
Irving Louis Horowitz	*Taking Lives: Genocide and State Power.* New Brunswick, NJ: Transaction, 1997.
Matthew Jardine	*East Timor: Genocide in Paradise.* Tucson, AZ: Odonian Press, 1995.
Fergal Keane	*Season of Blood: A Rwandan Journey.* New York: Viking Penguin, 1997.
Elizabeth Kemf, ed.	*The Law of the Mother: Protecting Indigenous Peoples in Protected Areas.* San Francisco, CA: Sierra Club Books, 1993.

Benjamin Kiernan — *The Pol Pot Regime: Race, Power, and Genocide in Cambodia Under the Khmer Rouge, 1975–79.* New Haven, CT: Yale University Press, 1998.

Richard M. Lerner — *Final Solutions: Biology, Prejudice, and Genocide.* University Park: Pennsylvania State University Press, 1992.

Eric Markusen and David Kopf — *The Holocaust and Strategic Bombing: Genocide and Total War in the 20th Century.* Boulder, CO: Westview, 1995.

Robert Melson — *Revolution and Genocide: On the Origins of the Armenian Genocide and the Holocaust.* Chicago: University of Chicago Press, 1996.

Martha Minow — *Between Vengeance and Forgiveness: Facing History After Genocide and Mass Violence.* Boston: Beacon, 1998.

Aryeh Neier — *War Crimes: Brutality, Genocide, Terror, and the Struggle for Justice.* New York: Times Books, 1998.

Jack Nusan Porter, ed. — *Genocide and Human Rights: A Global Anthology.* Lanham, MD: University Press of America, 1982.

Gerard Prunier — *The Rwandan Crisis: History of a Genocide.* New York: Columbia University Press, 1995.

Michael P. Scharf — *Balkan Justice: The Story Behind the First International War Crimes Trial Since Nuremberg.* Durham, NC: Carolina Academic Press, 1997.

Tsering Shakya — *The Dragon in the Land of Snows: A History of Modern Tibet Since 1947.* New York: Columbia University Press, 1999.

Roger W. Smith, ed. — *Genocide: Essays Toward Understanding, Early Warning, and Prevention.* Williamsburg, VA: Association of Genocide Scholars, 1999.

Periodicals

Brad Adams — "No Compromise for Khmer Rouge," *World Press Review,* June 2000.

Omer Bartov — "Defining Enemies, Making Victims: Germans, Jews, and the Holocaust," *American Historical Review,* June 1998. Available from the American Historical Association, Indiana University, 914 Atwater Ave., Bloomington, IN 47401.

Liberato C. Bautista — "The Case for an International Criminal Court," *Christian Social Action,* July/August 1998. Available from 100 Maryland Ave. NE, Washington DC 20002.

Barry Bennett — "The Holocaust: Denial and Memory," *Humanist,* May 15, 1997.

John R. Bolton — "Courting Danger: What's Wrong with the International Criminal Court," *National Interest,* Winter 1998/1999.

Jo-Marie Burt — "Time for a U.S. Truth Commission," *NACLA Report on the Americas,* May/June 1999.

| Jimmy Carter | "For an International Criminal Court," *New Perspectives Quarterly*, Winter 1997. |

| John Corry | "A Formula for Genocide," *American Spectator*, September 1998. |

| Christopher Hitchens | "Genocide and the Body-Baggers," *Nation*, November 29, 1999. |

| D'Arcy Jenish | "Preventable Genocide: International Community Failed to Prevent Rwandan Genocide," *Maclean's*, July 17, 2000. |

| Sebastian Junger | "Kosovo's Valley of Death," *Vanity Fair*, July 1998. |

| Alan J. Kuperman | "Rwanda in Retrospect," *Foreign Affairs*, January/February 2000. |

| Robert Melson | "Paradigms of Genocide: The Holocaust, the Armenian Genocide, and Contemporary Mass Destructions," *Annals of the American Academy of Political and Social Science*, November 1996. |

| John Milloy | "When a Language Dies," *Index on Censorship*, July/August 1999. |

| Damir Mirković | "Ethnic Conflict and Genocide: Reflections on Ethnic Cleansing in the Former Yugoslavia," *Annals of the American Academy of Political and Social Science*, November 1996. |

| Kingsley Chiedu Moghalu | "The Indictment of Milosevic: A Revolution in Human Rights," *New Perspectives Quarterly*, Summer 1999. |

| Donald Ottenhoff | "Genocide in Our Time," *Christian Century*, February 21, 1996. |

| John Pilger | "We Helped Them Descend Into Hell: U.S. and British Role in East Timor's Oppression," *New Statesman*, September 13, 1999. |

| Peter Schneider | "Saving Konrad Latte," *New York Times Magazine*, February 13, 2000. |

| *Unesco Courier* | "Building Blocks of International Justice," December 1999. |

| Stephen Weissman | "Living with Genocide," *Tikkun*, July/August 1997. |

| Kevin Whitelaw | "A Mission to Cambodia," *U.S. News & World Report*, May 8, 2000. |

| George S. Yacoubain Jr. | "The Efficacy of International Criminal Justice: Evaluating the Aftermath of the Rwandan Genocide," *World Affairs*, Spring 1999. |

| Howard Zinn | "Respecting the Holocaust," *Progressive*, November 1999. |

INDEX